JOURNAL FOR THE STUDY OF THE OLD TESTAMENT
SUPPLEMENT SERIES
13

Editors

David J A Clines

Philip R Davies

Department of Biblical Studies

The University of Sheffield

Sheffield S10 2TN

England

ISAIAH AND THE DELIVERANCE OF JERUSALEM

A Study of the Interpretation
of Prophecy in the Old Testament

R.E.CLEMENTS

Journal for the Study of the Old Testament
Supplement Series,13

ISSN 0309–0787
ISBN 0 905774 23 X

Published by
JSOT Press
Department of Biblical Studies
The University of Sheffield
Sheffield S10 2TN
England

Printed in Great Britain by
Redwood Burn Ltd., Trowbridge, Wiltshire

CONTENTS

PREFACE

The five lectures presented here were originally given under the auspices of the David S. Schaff Foundation in Pittsburgh Theological Seminary during the period 18-21st April, 1978. I am greatly indebted to the Trustees of the Foundation for the invitation to give these lectures and to President W.H. Kadel, Professor Jared J. Jackson and other members of the Faculty for their kind hospitality and interest. Three of the lectures were also delivered in University College, Cardiff during the period 14-16th February, 1978. I am appreciative of the encouragement received on that occasion and of numerous points of assistance offered by Professor H.W.F. Saggs.

The subject covered in these lectures may appear a rather over-worked one in recent years, since it is not long since Professor B.S. Childs' monograph Isaiah and the Assyrian Crisis (London, 1967) was published. No major new archaeological evidence relating to the threat to Jerusalem posed by the Assyrians in 701 B.C. has come to light in recent years. Yet the inconclusiveness of earlier studies has led me to believe that there is room for a further attempt on the problem. More particularly in the context of recent research, the relationship of that event to the preaching of Isaiah has aroused an increasing amount of attention. In one feature especially the perspective has changed markedly in the past few years by further investigation into the origin of a number of sayings in the book of the prophet Isaiah which have been widely used to highlight that prophet's expectation of the outcome of the threat posed by Sennacherib. I am especially indebted to Dr Hermann Barth for making available to me a copy of his dissertation on these passages, which has now been published as Die Jesaja-Worte in der Josiazeit. Israel und Assur als Thema einer produktiven Neuinterpretation der Jesajaüberlieferung (Neukirchen-Vluyn, 1978). This enabled me to consult his work much earlier than would otherwise have been the case.

My interest in this particular problem of historical and theological concern to Old Testament prophecy was initially occasioned by the invitation to contribute a commentary on Isaiah 1-39 in the series New Century Bible. The delay in the appearance of that volume which my diversion to deal with these specific problems has occasioned is something for which I must apologise. At the same time, to any student familiar with recent studies of the prophet Isaiah, it will be clear that the resolution of the issues dealt with in these lectures has a very far-reaching effect upon the overall interpretation of the prophetic book. I hope therefore that the delay may be forgiven, and that the necessarily concise treatment in the following pages may occasion sufficient interest in the larger work when it appears.

R.E. Clements
Cambridge
October, 1979

Chapter 1

SENNACHERIB AND JERUSALEM

In 1878 there was published posthumously a translation by the distinguished pioneer orientalist George Smith of a text which had been acquired by the British Museum more than thirty years before /1/. It was a version of the royal annals of the Assyrian ruler Sennacherib (704-681 B.C.), of which a number of other editions are now known to exist /2/. It contained an extended account of Sennacherib's attack upon Judah in 701 B.C., and mentioned in detail the surrender and tribute paid by the Judean king Hezekiah who had rebelled against his Assyrian suzerain. Hence it provides extensive external corroboration and amplification of the account of this submission which the Old Testament provides us with in 2 Kings 18:13-16. In a dramatic fashion it has presented a splendid example of the way in which the skills of archaeologists and linguists have served to illuminate the text of the Bible. At the same time this ancient cuneiform text, and the related versions of it which have been subsequently found, have raised problems and questions which have so far received anything but unanimous answers from scholars. This is because the Old Testament contains a further narrative of Sennacherib's threat to Jerusalem in 2 Kings 18:17-19:37, which describes a very different outcome to the confrontation, and which makes no mention of Hezekiah's surrender. In fact it concludes with a dramatic comment telling how the angel of Yahweh slew 185,000 soldiers of the Assyrian army in one night (2 Kings 19:35). Is this fact or fiction? If it is fiction, how has such an interpretation of the situation arisen in view of the evident clarity with which Judah's own state archives recalled Hezekiah's surrender? After a century of scholarly research and a number of major studies devoted to the subject, besides a host of lesser articles and of commentaries on the passages relating to it, it may appear that we are no nearer a solution, for wide disagreement still exists. Yet by worrying at the problem in this way, and even by highlighting the different solutions which are still canvassed, scholarship has moved a long way nearer to obtaining a truly convincing resolution of the problem. At least it is arguable that new methods of biblical criticism, new ways of approaching the problem, and above all a strenuous effort to evaluate the nature and reliability of the evidence, have made a further attempt at understanding the biblical material worthwhile.

Two factors may be adduced in support of such a venture of biblical interpretation. The first may be clarified by citing some concluding remarks from B.S. Childs' relatively recent study entitled Isaiah and the Assyrian Crisis: "In terms of the specific historical problem of 701, it seems unlikely that a satisfactory historical solution will be forthcoming without fresh extra-biblical evidence" /4/. Undoubtedly it is true that the situation could be clarified if we were to have available more extra-biblical evidence regarding Sennacherib's attack upon Judah in 701.

Yet to put the problem in this fashion, and especially to put the historical problem first, is, as Childs' further remarks show, to see the problem in a rather heavily historicist perspective. We are, in reality, remarkably well informed about the events of 701 so far as Assyria and Judah are concerned, and we know a great deal more about this event than about many others of Judah's stormy history. We shall, of course, never know all that we should like about what took place in that year. The problem exists because the Old Testament tells us about a remarkable deliverance of Jerusalem from Sennacherib, apparently in that year, which lacks external corroboration. One possible solution to the problem is to dismiss this narrative as legend, of more interest to the theologian than the historian. If this view is correct, then it is clear that no amount of further external information about Sennacherib's campaign in 701 will ever resolve the problem for us. What we need is some insight into the nature and origin of this "legend" in order to show us how it arose, and what purpose it was intended to serve. From the historical point of view therefore we may assert that we know much of what happened in 701. The possibility that something of a remarkable and dramatic nature, which is not mentioned in Sennacherib's annals, happened to the Assyrian army then is only one among a number of possible

10

explanations which may account for the lengthy Old Testament narrative. It may be that we can discover other factors which will show us how and why this narrative arose and why it gives such a highly coloured picture of events. To conclude, as many recent scholars have done, that 2 Kings 18:17-19:37 refers to a quite separate incident, most probably at some later time than 701, is itself a highly questionable way out of the difficulty /5/. Only if it proves totally impossible to understand this narrative in relation to what we already know about the events of 701 could we regard this hypothesis as a satisfactory way of resolving the problem. Yet it is largely because of the popularity of such a "second campaign" hypothesis that the lure of hoping for additional extra-biblical evidence has remained so attractive. If there were only one campaign, and if Sennacherib's annals fully report this, then we have all the evidence that we can properly hope for so far as the historical situation is concerned. Our problems can then be seen to be essentially literary and theological, since they must, first of all, be concerned with understanding the narrative record in the Old Testament which sees the confrontation between Sennacherib and Hezekiah in a very different perspective from that adopted by the Assyrian annals.

We may take it to be our primary aim therefore to understand the literary origin of the Isaiah narrative of 2 Kings 18:17-19:37, and to evaluate it, not simply from the point of view of its factual veracity, but from the point of view of its theological ideas and its source of origin. As soon as we do this we are confronted by the fact that the problem becomes more important than we may at first have supposed. The theological ideas of this narrative are among the leading theological motifs which have governed the writing of the entire narrative history of Israel and Judah under the monarchy, for this focuses upon two major institutions: the royal dynasty of David and the special significance of Jerusalem among all the cities of Israel. Another theological aspect of the problem may also be highlighted, since it has a bearing upon the wider biblical perspective regarding belief in divine providence. The report that the dire consequences threatened by the confrontation between Sennacherib and Hezekiah were averted by direct divine intervention is highly unusual in Old Testament history-writing. In consequence it has often been cited as a biblical example of the technique of resolving human historical tragedies by resort to a <u>Deus ex machina</u>. It portrays a kind of "absoluteness" about divine providence which is very untypical of the Old Testament as a whole, and which two and half millennia of further history, most especially Jewish history, show to be unwarranted. Historical disasters, even for the people of God, have not been averted by the sudden intervention of the angel of Yahweh. It is important for us therefore to see the way in which the Old Testament itself sets this particular belief about providence in perspective.

We may begin our survey of the nature of the problem by noting the content of the relevant part of Sennacherib's annals:

As to Hezekiah, the Jew, he did not submit to my yoke, I laid siege to 46 of his strong cities, walled forts and to the countless small villages in their vicinity, and conquered (them) by means of well-stamped (earth-) ramps, and battering-rams brought (thus) near (to the walls) (combined with) the attack by foot soldiers, (using) mines, breeches as well as sapper work. I drove out (of them) 200,150 people, young and old, male and female, horses, mules, donkeys, camels, big and small cattle beyond counting, and considered (them) booty. Himself I made a prisoner in Jerusalem, his royal residence, like a bird in a cage. I surrounded him with earthwork in order to molest those who were leaving his city's gate. His towns which I had plundered, I took away from his country and gave them (over) to Mitinti, king of Ashdod, Padi, king of Ekron, and Sillibel, king of Gaza. Thus I reduced his country, but I still increased the tribute and the katrû-presents (due) to me (as his) overlord which I imposed (later) upon him beyond the former tribute, to be delivered annually. Hezekiah himself, who the terror-inspiring splendour of my lordship had over-whelmed, and whose irregular and elite troops which he had brought into Jerusalem, his royal residence, in order to strengthen (it), had deserted him, did send me, later, to Nineveh, my lordly city, together with 30 talents of gold, 800 talents of silver, precious stones, antimony, large cuts of red stone, couches (inlaid) with ivory, nîmedu-chairs (inlaid) with ivory, elephant-hides, ebony wood, boxwood (and) all kinds of valuable treasures, his (own) daughters, concubines, male and female musicians. In order to deliver the tribute and to do obeisance as a slave he sent his (personal) messenger /6/.

In all essentials the report given here can be reconciled with that given in 2 Kings 18:13-16:

In the fourteenth year of king Hezekiah Sennacherib king of Assyria came up against all the fortified cities of Judah and took them. And Hezekiah king of Judah sent to the king of Assyria at Lachish, saying, "I have done wrong; withdraw from me; whatever you impose on me I will bear". And the king of Assyria required of Hezekiah king of Judah three hundred talents of silver and thirty talents of gold. And Hezekiah gave him all the silver that was found in the house of Yahweh, and in the treasuries of the king's house. At that time Hezekiah stripped the gold from the doors of the temple of Yahweh, and from the doorposts which Hezekiah king of Judah had overlaid and gave it to the king of Assyria.

In spite of the heading set to the translation in J.B. Pritchard's Ancient Near Eastern Texts, "The Siege of Jerusalem", it is evident that there was no full-scale siege of the city, although the preparations were made for one. Jerusalem was isolated by means of an earthen defence-wall, and Sennacherib controlled all access to the city and egress from it. Apparently Hezekiah surrendered to the Assyrian king at Lachish (cf. 2 Kings 18:14), before the siege proper was tightly pressed, but already after a large number of the Judean defenders had deserted. The arrogant tone of the Assyrian account should not mislead us into supposing that it is in serious factual error. Similarly the lack of any explicit mention of a siege in 2 Kings 18:13-16 may be taken to give an adequate perspective and we cannot suppose that the Assyrian record is referring to a siege that took place subsequent to Hezekiah's initial surrender.

In his dissertation of 1926 L.L. Honor lists six possible explanations for what actually happened in 701 and how we may account for the Old Testament narrative of a significant last-minute deliverance of Jerusalem /7/. For the sake of brevity we may eliminate minor variations and reduce these to three main possibilities:

Isaiah and the Deliverance of Jerusalem

(1) The biblical account given in 2 Kings 18:17-19:37, generally referred to as account B, is a late legendary version of what happened in 701, of which a more accurate historical picture is afforded by the Assyrian annals and the report of Hezekiah's surrender in 2 Kings 18:13-16. This latter narrative has generally come to be known as account A. All three accounts therefore refer to the same event.

(2) The biblical account B (2 Kings 18:17-19:37) refers to a subsequent siege of Jerusalem by Sennacherib, which took place shortly after Hezekiah's submission described in account A (2 Kings 18:13-16). The assumption is then made that something happened to make Sennacherib regret his leniency to Hezekiah, and attempt to take Jerusalem by force in spite of the Judean king's surrender. In this effort Sennacherib was unexpectedly thwarted by circumstances which we do not clearly know. Hence accounts A and B do not refer to the same event and the Assyrian record refers only to the surrender of account A.

(3) The biblical account B refers to a siege of Jerusalem which took place during a subsequent campaign by Sennacherib, of which no record is preserved in the Assyrian annals. This is therefore a modification of the second hypothesis, with the assumption that as much as a decade may separate the events of the biblical accounts A and B.

The first of these hypotheses is in many respects the simplest, since it makes all three major sources of knowledge refer to essentially the same event which took place in 701. The second and third hypotheses are weak because they depend upon the assumption that a second attempt to take Jerusalem was made by Sennacherib, either later in 701, or later still in the furtherance of some other campaign. The complete lack of evidence from Assyrian sources that there was such a second attempt to take the city renders these hypotheses very insecure, since they rest entirely upon a particular interpretation of account B. In the one case we must accept that there is sufficient connection between accounts A and B to conclude that they are reconcilable with each other as variant interpretations of the same event. In the other case we are forced to conclude that the two accounts cannot be reconciled with each other, but that there is a sufficient measure of reliability attaching to account B to lead us to believe that it is referring to a later event.

One: Sennacherib and Jerusalem

Evidently therefore a great deal depends upon our making a clear assessment of the nature and historical veracity of account B. This may then be recognised to be a major task which we must undertake.

However the historical problem is only one aspect of the difficulty created by the narrative of the deliverance of Jerusalem in 2 Kings 18:17-19:37. As this narrative stands it presents the prophet Isaiah as foretelling that Sennacherib's attempt to take Jerusalem would fail, and as assuring Hezekiah that he had nothing to fear from the Assyrians since Yahweh his God was with him. The account therefore is an important point of interpretation for the preaching of Isaiah, and is all the more interesting because the particular sayings ascribed to him are not found repeated in the book of Isaiah. Yet there are, scattered throughout the first part of the book, several sayings of a distinctive character that have been thought to fit very appropriately as comparable messages of assurance that Jerusalem would be defended by God. They foretell that the Assyrians would be dramatically and suddenly overthrown by the hand of God. It is impossible therefore to describe the picture of Isaiah's preaching given in account B as a false one, and to dismiss the prophecies it contains as unconnected with the book which now bears the prophet's name.

Furthermore the question must inevitably be raised, even if suspicion still hovers over the issue of the reliability of the narrative of 2 Kings 18:17-19:37, what the prophecies in the book of Isaiah which foretell the overthrow of the Assyrians have to do with this narrative. It could be that it is the existence of these prophecies which have given rise to the narrative portrayal, so that this latter is in fact the product of a conviction that such prophecies must have been fulfilled. Conversely it could be that the reverse is true and that the narrative has encouraged the addition of oracles setting out rather traditional affirmations of divine protection to the collection of Isaiah's prophecies. Yet a third possibility is that both the "deliverance" oracles in the book of Isaiah and the narrative account B have originated from the same circles and were intended to be understood in conjunction with each other. In this case we are evidently not dealing with an isolated "legend" which presented a rather over-dramatised interpretation of one particular historical event,

15

but with a more widely entrenched conviction that was closely related to the prophet Isaiah and his preaching. In any case this evaluation of the material in both the prophecies and the narrative must be made, since we have already pointed out that the main theological affirmations of the narrative are to be found quite extensively expressed elsewhere in the Old Testament. These affirm specifically that Yahweh is quite uniquely concerned for Jerusalem, more than any other city of Israel, and that this concern is directly related to his support for the dynasty of David. In fact it is evident upon close examination that the incident reported by the narrative of account B, the deliverance of Jersusalem from Sennacherib, forms a kind of high-point in the whole story of the monarchy which begins in 1 Sam. 8 and does not conclude until 2 Kings 25. The interest in Jerusalem which reappears frequently in this history, which is designated as the place where Yahweh "has chosen to set his name" (1 Kings 8:29 etc.) comes to its fullest justification in the story of the city's rescue out of the very grip of Sennacherib. Moreover this story makes the very greatest measure of theological play over what happened, by describing the blasphemous boasts of the Assyrian king which he was unable to fulfil.

A further factor makes the analysis of this theological motif a very far-reaching one so far as the literature and theology of the Old Testament are concerned. There are in certain psalms, viz. Pss. 46, 48 and 76, a series of poetic portrayals in which the city of Jerusalem is represented as being attacked by unnamed enemies who are defeated by God. The victory is quite exclusively his, but the foes that he defeats are rather loosely described as "kings", "nations" or "kingdoms". Their overthrow is a victory for justice and righteousness on behalf of the entire people of God. This "Conflict with the Nations" motif is directly associated with Jerusalem, and shows evident connections with a far older range of traditions about the protection of God for his divine residence (temple) from the ancient Near East. It has come quite widely to be accepted as a central part of what several scholars have called the "Zion tradition", and has been thought to be far older than the time of Isaiah /8/. Thus the prophet could himself have been deeply influenced by the tradition regarding Yahweh's special protection for "Zion",

16

and this influence could have determined the language of his prophecies, and even his expectation about the deliverance of Jerusalem. Against this we should note that for long scholars argued in a reverse direction and concluded that the assurances of Yahweh's protection for Jerusalem, and his overthrow of his enemies there, grew up on the basis of what took place when Hezekiah confronted Sennacherib /9/. In either case, it is evident that the motif of the protection of Zion which comes to the forefront in the narrative account of the city's deliverance from the Assyrians in 701 bears some relationship to the "Conflict with the Nations" motif of the Psalms, and to the belief that this once formed part of a comprehensive "Zion tradition". In several respects therefore it may be argued that the historical problem of determining what actually happened in 701 and the question of the historical reliability of account B of 2 Kings 18:17-19:37 form only a part of a much wider theological problem. The study of this narrative can lead us into one of the central theological themes of the Old Testament.

It may be appropriate at this point to raise a broader aspect of the question of the relationship of historical writing to events in the Bible. For more than a century the writing of a "history of Israel" has been accepted as a major critical undertaking towards gaining an insight into the life and world from which the Old Testament arose. This is perfectly proper and appropriate, and has contributed greatly to a fuller grasp of the nature of the Bible and the world in which it originated. At the same time the pursuit of such an undertaking has inevitably drawn greatest attention towards those parts of the Old Testament which are historical in form, and particularly to those parts of this history which are most directly factual and which thereby provide the best evidence for reconstructing the history of Israel. The far greater critical preference for, and interest in, the books of 1 and 2 Kings, over against 1 and 2 Chronicles, is a natural consequence of this. At the same time we must remember that the study of the history of Israel is intended as an aid towards interpreting the Old Testament, and not the other way round. Hence those parts of the Old Testament literature which are less positively historical, or which stand at a much greater distance from the events which they recount, may also be of great importance in other ways. Historicity is not the only category by which narrative is to be valued and interpreted. Certainly it is also clear from critical examination that there is a great unevenness between the various parts of the Old Testament, even those parts which are in the form of historical narrative, in respect of the closeness of the narrative to events. This is certainly true of the books of 1 and 2 Kings which display considerable variation in this respect. At the same time those other parts which stand at a greater distance from events may be particularly revealing about the ideas and institutions by which the men and women who were the actors in this history saw their world being influenced. This is particularly true of the stories which concern the origin of the monarchy as an institution (1 Sam. 8-12; 15-16). It is very difficult to determine how far these stories accurately report events that actually took place, but they nevertheless bring out a great wealth of insight regarding the way in which men viewed the monarchy as an institution. In a very fundamental way therefore they present an insight into the way in which men viewed their historical experience and regarded those religious and political institutions which affected their lives and determined their destiny. So also may this be true in regard to the accounts of what happened in 701. It is clear in any case that the theological resort to a description of the action of "the angel of Yahweh" can only be an interpretation of an event which the historian must necessarily understand and describe differently.

We may proceed in the light of these remarks to make some preliminary survey of the material that is available for the clarification of our problems, and to offer some suggestions about how we should proceed to tackle them. We may begin by suggesting that the historical side of the problem is less prominent and less pressing than has frequently been held to be the case. So far as the question of what happened in 701 is concerned we have a reasonably clear picture. After rebelling against his Assyrian suzerain by withholding the payment of tribute Hezekiah found himself confronted with a punitive force of Assyrian soldiers who arrived in Judah to re-assert their control over the land. In deciding to withhold tribute Hezekiah had come to rely very heavily upon a treaty-alliance with Egypt in which assurances of mutual support in the almost inevitable event of an

Assyrian attack were made. It is also clear that the Philistine cities of Ashdod, Ekron and Gaza were involved, apparently by the removal and imprisonment of their pro-Assyrian vassal-kings.

The exact sequence of events cannot be determined with certainty from the Assyrian records, since this does not necessarily adhere to a strict chronological order, but deals with countries and regions one by one.

After the major part of Judah had been ravaged and destroyed (the annals of Sennacherib mention no less than forty-six towns and cities), Jerusalem was threatened with a siege and preparations were made for this. However the inevitable and horrifying consequences of siege were averted by Hezekiah's surrender to the Assyrians before any attack on Jerusalem was pressed home. Virtually alone among the cities of Judah therefore Jerusalem escaped a battle, the horrors of a prolonged siege, or any serious destruction. Hezekiah had submitted in time to avert a holocaust. The terms that were imposed upon the king of Judah have often been interpreted as surprisingly lenient, since he retained his throne and his status as a client vassal. This could be so, although we can only speculate why this should have been the case. The major suggestion has been that the necessity for preparations to meet an attack by the Egyptians forced Sennacherib to accept a quick settlement and hence to offer moderate terms. However the Assyrian annals suggest that the Egyptians had already been defeated by this time at Eltekeh, and that the Philistine cities had already been re-established with their pro-Assyrian vassal-rulers.

Certainly on the other side it is easy to exaggerate the supposed leniency of the surrender terms that were imposed on Hezekiah. They were severe enough, and in retrospect it is clear that, whatever the terms were in regard to details, one factor stands out as of over-riding importance. This was the decision to allow Hezekiah to retain his client-vassal status. It is most likely that this marks the determination of the Assyrians to adhere to a policy that had already been decided upon long before, going back to the time of Ahaz. In 732 Judah had been deprived of part of its territory, as now occurred yet again in 701, and had been organised as a vassal-state under a native ruler. On the other hand the Northern Kingdom of Israel, after an attempt at such an arrangement in 732, had been incorporated directly into the Assyrian provincial system in 722, with no such native vassal ruler on its throne /10/. Since we can only speculate as to the reason for this difference of treatment between the two kingdoms, one factor immediately comes to mind. The Northern Kingdom, once Jehu's dynasty had come to an end in 746, had no such stabilising dynastic tradition such as Judah enjoyed under the Davidides. Is it not likely that the Assyrians, who had every reason for wanting to maintain a firm and stable government in the various territories of their empire, should have decided to adhere to the policy whenever possible of using powerful native princes, whose effectiveness owed much to their place within a respected dynasty of kings? We may couple this with another feature of Assyrian policy which marked a difference between the treatment of the two kingdoms of Judah and Israel. Once the immediate situation of the defeats and surrenders to which the two kingdoms submitted was past, one long term consequence began to reveal itself. The erstwhile Northern Kingdom of Israel was subjected to what the orientalist H. Donner has called the "third phase" of Assyrian imperial domination /11/. This was the wholesale depopulation of provincial territories, and the replacement of native peoples by others uprooted from elsewhere in the Assyrian empire. This was something very different from the taking away as prisoners of soldiers and notable citizens, which is mentioned in Sennacherib's Annals. It is clear that, so far as Israel was concerned, such deportations continued to take place well into the following century, bringing about extended social and political disturbance. Judah, restricted as it was in territory, escaped such a fate under its vassal king and as a consequence of its separate political status as a client state /12/.

Overall therefore we may claim that the supposed leniency in Sennacherib's treatment of Hezekiah in 701 has been more than a little exaggerated, and there is no great difficulty for us in piecing together a coherent picture of what happened as a consequence of Hezekiah's negotiations for a treaty with Egypt and his decision to withdraw support from Assyria in the years 705-701. If we combine the evidence of 2 Kings 18:13-16 with that supplied externally from Sennacherib's annals the facts fit together tolerably smoothly and coherently. Hezekiah's rebellion evoked strong reaction from

One: Sennacherib and Jerusalem

Assyria, and Egypt's help proved vain. Hezekiah saw almost his entire country ravaged, with virtually every town destroyed except his capital of Jerusalem. Once further resistance was clearly useless he surrendered before the siege of Jerusalem was pressed, and he had to accept the terms that were offered. Our embarrassment is caused, not by the lack of information, but by the fact that the narrative of 2 Kings 18:17-19:37 does not appear to fit within this framework of events. The main difficulty therefore is occasioned by the contents of this narrative which we call account B, and the need to understand how it has arisen and how it relates to the events of 701. Within its present setting there is nothing to suggest that it belongs to some other Assyrian campaign than that of the years 705-701.From the point of view of method, therefore, we may return to the point which we have already made previously. Before any other conclusions are drawn from it about any further Assyrian threats to Jerusalem either in 701 or later, we must examine this narrative itself, and evaluate its merits as a source of historical information. In this regard we may make the following preliminary points:

1. The narrative is self-evidently not from a time closely contemporaneous with the events it describes, since it concludes with a mention of the circumstances of Sennacherib's death, which did not take place until 681 B.C.

2. In form and content it further betrays the fact that it has been composed at some interval after the events it describes. It is a piece of "narrative theology", rather than a historical narrative proper, and has clearly been woven together from two roughly parallel accounts (usually termed B1 and B2). Its explanation for the event which forms its climax is dramatically theological in character. This is the reference to the work of "the angel of Yahweh" in 2 Kings 19:35 in killing 185,000 Assyrian soldiers. All too readily those scholars who have sought to use this narrative as a historical source have assumed that we can rationalise this reference and refer it to some plague, or other threat, which hindered Sennacherib. Such rationalising explanations of biblical narratives are merely guesses, which do little to assist a proper understanding of how such affirmations have arisen.

21

3. We may also insist that there is an inherent improbability in supposing that in a subsequent campaign of which we have no independent information, events took a startlingly similar course to those of 701 up to the point when Hezekiah surrendered. In this later siege of Jerusalem, however, when the king of Judah did not submit to the Assyrian king, events took a markedly different turn. Hezekiah was delivered and the Assyrians withdrew for no known reason. Such is the conclusion of those scholars who accept that the narrative account B refers to a later Assyrian campaign, perhaps as late as 688 B.C. Only the surest of evidence could lead us to conclude that such a remarkable repetition of events occurred, and such sure evidence is lacking.

4. If we take the apparently more plausible option, that after Hezekiah's surrender to Sennacherib in 701, the Assyrian king relented of his supposed leniency and tried, in contradiction of his own agreed terms, to force an entry into Jerusalem and to humiliate Hezekiah further then we also run into comparable historical difficulties. There are both psychological and military considerations which tell heavily against such a reconstruction of events and the claim to Assyrian leniency is almost certainly mistaken. If the situation had appeared sufficiently hopeless to Hezekiah before his surrender to Sennacherib to make further resistance futile, how much more would this have been so after his surrender had taken place. Hezekiah had lost almost all his troops and there would have been no opportunity whatsoever for the city to have replenished its food supply, nor to have recovered its morale. Furthermore, there is evidence from the prophet Isaiah that the populace of the city was in no mood to face once again an even tougher threat from Assyria. In fact this attempt to reconstruct a situation in which Sennacherib made a second unsuccessful siege on Jerusalem in 701 is every bit as implausible and unlikely as the theory of a second unrecorded Assyrian campaign later. We may conclude provisionally therefore that we do have a reasonably clear picture of what took place in 701, and that our major problem is to obtain some understanding of the remarkable narrative of 2 Kings 18:17-19:37 which pictures the events of that year in such an unexpected and extraordinary way. Only if we are totally

unable to account for this narrative within this framework should we have to return to consider once again the possibility that it was not originally concerned with the events of that fateful year at all.

From the point of view of method, however, we should do well to try to reach some conclusions on another issue before analysing in detail the structure and theological interests of this much discussed narrative. What was the attitude of Isaiah to these events? Can we find support in the preserved prophecies of this important figure to indicate that he did adopt a strongly encouraging and reassuring stance towards Hezekiah and his attempt to resist the Assyrians? The earlier critical view of the preaching of this prophet failed to reach any clear consensus on this point, the more radical commentators denying to Isaiah those passages which might have been held to illustrate such a position, and the more conservative critics defending their authenticity. Yet even for these latter a great difficulty had to be faced since it was also clear that Isaiah had uttered some dramatically threatening words to Hezekiah and to Judah generally. It was then necessary to explain when and why the prophet had changed his position and had turned his threats into firm prophecies of assurance and deliverance. In any case, if it is clear, or even reasonably probable, that Isaiah had prophesied of Jerusalem's deliverance in 701 then we should have available a valuable source of comparison with the picture presented of that prophet in the historical narrative. More than this, however, we should almost certainly have to hand the most plausible explanation of how the narrative of the city's deliverance had arisen. If the prophet had assured his king and people that they would be delivered by their God from the hands of the Assyrian tormentors, then it is not too difficult to believe that the inference should have been drawn, even if mistakenly, that such a deliverance had taken place. The belief that a prophecy would be fulfilled could so easily have been turned into a belief that it had been fulfilled.

There is, however, yet a further complicating factor. More than half a century ago S. Mowinckel argued that the story of Jerusalem's deliverance had arisen, not on the basis of prophecies of Isaiah, but on the basis of a far older tradition which was ultimately mythological in its origin /13/. This tradition is to be found reflected in Pss. 46, 48 and 76, and is, so Mowinckel believed, an Israelite adaptation of the ancient Near Eastern myth of the conflict of the Creator God with the unruly forces of chaos and disorder which threatened his universe. Increasingly the view has gained wide currency among scholars that this particular motif of Yahweh's "Conflict with the Nations" is of ancient origin and antedates the story of how Jerusalem was miraculously delivered in 701. Far from these psalms being a reflection of the events of that year, therefore, the story of these events has been taken to be a reflection of the content of these psalms. Yet even this position, attractive as it is in many ways as an explanation of how the narrative of Jerusalem's deliverance came to be written, really forces us back to consider first of all the evidence from the prophet Isaiah. If the authors of the narrative account had been deeply affected by the hymnic affirmations of these psalms that Jerusalem would be uniquely protected by Yahweh, why should Isaiah the prophet not himself have been so affected? In fact, with his traditio-historical methodology, this is precisely the position adopted by G. von Rad, which has had a very far-reaching influence upon a whole range of studies and interpretations of the prophet /14/. We are then, even if we accept the conclusion that these psalms, or at least their central affirmation, are very much older than the time of Isaiah's prophesying, compelled to consider first of all what the content of this latter was.

We may insist also that a very great deal more hinges on this prior question about the message of Isaiah in its relation to the events of 701 B.C. than may at first appear. The greatness of Isaiah as a prophet has been widely acclaimed, not least by G. von Rad /15/. Yet this is coupled by him, somewhat strangely, with the belief that ultimately he was a disappointed man /16/. His message had been rejected and ignored, so that neither Hezekiah nor Judah more generally had risen to the heights of faith to which Isaiah had called them. When summoned to display a dramatically bold act of faith in Yahweh, Hezekiah had declined, and had instead abjectly submitted himself and his kingdom to the cruel mercy of the Assyrians. The prophet saw his people failing to rise to the level of trust in God to which he had summoned them. Whether this is a fair and true picture of Isaiah will require to be examined, but it raises some very searching questions about the nature of faith itself. Several commentators have branded the particular act of religious faith demanded by Isaiah as a kind of irrational "Utopianism" /17/. If Isaiah had called to heroic faith in resisting the Assyrians, and Hezekiah had refused to heed this call, are we to conclude that Hezekiah's surrender was simply a sign of his own want of faith? /18/. Would events have turned out otherwise if he had refused to submit? The very fact that we have a serious problem in determining the historical veracity of the account of Jerusalem's deliverance shows how hard it is to arrive at any easy solution. In fact we may argue that the belief that Isaiah did affirm such a remarkable degree of assurance and protection for Jerusalem in a moment of exceptional crisis raises as many problems as it solves. It is undoubtedly true that it would enable us to accept as authentic to Isaiah a number of passages in the prophetic book which bears his name. To this extent it resolves any need to look elsewhere to explain their origin. Yet it leaves us with an interpretation of Isaiah's message which cannot altogether escape the label of being "Utopian" and unrealistic. All the more would this be so if we were to accept, as von Rad and others so clearly seem to do, that the ultimate origin of this belief lay not with Isaiah himself, but with a far older tradition which was ultimately mythological in its nature. We cannot escape the historical fact that, little more than a century later, Jerusalem was twice in just over a decade faced with a threat from the Babylonians closely comparable to that posed earlier by Sennacherib. We know that on both occasions the city was ultimately forced into submission and no "angel of Yahweh" appeared from the skies to kill off the attacking forces. It is also clear that the faith that is reflected in the narrative of Jerusalem's deliverance in 701, and in such psalms as 46 and 48, may well have contributed in no little measure to the false expectations that Jerusalem would be secure from such defeat.

At that time the prophet Jeremiah and the authors of the book of Lamentations called their people to a far more difficult and courageous act of faith: to believe that the destruction of Jerusalem and the laying in ruins of its temple was an action ordered and ordained of God for the just punishment of his people. This was surely a far more searching and dangerous thing to do, since it is not difficult to accept that in the moment of supreme crisis God will intervene to rescue his people, however rarely such faith seems to be justified by events. What these later figures sought for was a faith that could comprehend not simply triumph and security, but disaster and suffering, within its range. Furthermore it is evident from the book of Lamentations that it was precisely the presence of the kind of reckless assurance engendered by the theme, if not the actual story, of Jerusalem's deliverance in 701 that made the fact of this subsequent downfall so hard to accept:

The kings of the earth did not believe,
    or any of the inhabitants of the world,
that foe or enemy could enter
    the gates of Jerusalem.

(Lam. 4:12).

It is surely a much more difficult article of faith to accept for oneself that failure and defeat may also have a part to play in the providence and purposes of God. Even if we conclude therefore, irrespective of how events actually turned out, that Isaiah had summoned Hezekiah and his kingdom to a bold and exceptional act of faith in defying Sennacherib in 701, would this not in the end lead us to a picture of Isaiah as an exceedingly dangerous and misleading kind of prophet? If, with G. Fohrer, we tone down to some extent the firmness and certainty of the prophet's note of assurance by arguing that it was throughout intended to be understood conditionally as dependent upon the people's repentance and genuine willingness to trust in God /19/, this does not really ease the problem. It merely leaves us with the notion of a kind of ideal faith which can subdue kingdoms and defeat armies, but which is of so rare a kind as to be impossible for ordinary people. Our knowledge of history and of the workings of divine providence shows us unmistakeably that angels do not come from heaven to slay the enemy. If we rationalise this element of the story and refer it to some other historical happening we do not really resolve our difficulty. We simply invent for ourselves an attractive hypothesis which excuses us from dealing with the more unpalatable feature of the biblical narrative. In fact the main burden of D. Bonhoeffer's summons that we should learn to live as men "come of age" is precisely this point about the nature of God's providence /20/.

One: Sennacherib and Jerusalem

The point I have already mentioned about the contrast between the narrative account of what happened in 701 and the much shorter and less theologically coloured record of what took place just over a century later in 598 and 587 B.C. points to an element of tension which exists in Old Testament history. Nor does this tension exist solely on the historical plane as an interesting contrast between what happened to Judah and Jerusalem when facing two of the great super-powers of the ancient world. It penetrates to a deeper level and points us to two types of faith: the faith that finds its object in security and deliverance and the faith that recognises, and can embrace, tragedy and judgement. For those who ultimately see the centre of all biblical history in the death and crucifixion of the one who came as the deliverer of Israel there is no question as to which type of faith can penetrate to a more profound level of human existence. We have a very genuine theological interest therefore in seeking to trace how the story of Jerusalem's deliverance in 701 was related to actual events, and how its confident note of assurance came to arise. It is also important to note how the very dangers of this assurance came quickly to be recognised and have been themselves linked directly to the story of that momentous year in Judah's history.

Chapter 2

ISAIAH AND THE THREAT TO JERUSALEM

In the preceding chapter we have endeavoured to establish a clear picture of what we know took place in the year 701 B.C., when Judah was severely ravaged by Sennacherib's army. The outstanding question that remains with us from the purely historical perspective is whether the fact that Jerusalem was spared then as a result of Hezekiah's timely surrender is a sufficient explanation for the highly theological narrative of 2 Kings 18:17-19:37, or whether this must be regarded as referring to some other confrontation between Hezekiah and the king of Assyria. However, before we can deal with this question effectively, we must ascertain what the attitude of the prophet Isaiah was to Hezekiah's rebellion against Assyria, and, if possible, to the actual situation when Jerusalem faced this particular threat, so far as we can learn this from the book of Isaiah. What has been bewildering for interpreters of the prophet is the presence in the book of apparently contradictory expressions of attitude, on the one hand sharply critical of Hezekiah's policy of rebellion, and on the other dramatically affirmative about the certainty of God's protection and of the overthrow of Judah's Assyrian attackers. Which is the correct picture of the prophet's word, or is it possible that they are both in some paradoxical way correct? Can we conclude that, at the last moment, and in spite of all the dire threats that had gone before, Isaiah suddenly changed his message to one of assurance with a clear promise of deliverance? /1/ The widely different approaches and conclusions that have appeared among commentators invite us to proceed cautiously, and suggest that a consistent and theologically satisfying interpretation cannot be reached easily.

In trying to sort out the difficulties much must depend on our ability to sift out secondary material from that which is primary. Useful as many guidelines of style and language may be, in the end it is the overall result which must prove convincing or not. Similarly the problem of assigning dates to sayings which are preserved without any explicit indication of what these may have been has to be acknowledged. We can only assign tentative dates and rely upon the emergence of a coherent and psychologically consistent account of Isaiah's preaching to assure ourselves that we have worked on sound principles. Since it is impossible to attempt a complete summary of Isaiah's preaching, we must content ourselves with answering a number of preliminary questions before we can address ourselves to the major one, which is that of determining whether the prophecies contained in the book of Isaiah which declare the sudden divine overthrow of the Assyrians come from the prophet or not /2/. The three prior questions which most concern us are: (1) What was Isaiah's attitude to Hezekiah's rebellion against Assyria in the years 705-701 B.C.? (2) What did he have to say to the inhabitants of Jerusalem in the year 701? (3) What was his message concerning the Assyrians as a conquering power? It is only when we have made up our minds about these issues that we can consider whether it is conceivable that Isaiah did foretell the defeat of the Assyrians outside Jerusalem in the year 701.

If, as a result of this study, we find that the picture given of Isaiah and his preaching in the narrative account B (2 Kings 18:17-19:37) is in line with what we otherwise know of him, then we should have a strong basis for accepting the evidence of the narrative as historically reliable. On the other hand, if we find some other explanation for the origin of these sayings in the book of Isaiah then we should certainly also have a good indication of the source from which the picture contained in the narrative has been drawn. It is simply inadequate to state that the portrayal of Isaiah in the narratives stands somewhere on the fringe of the prophet's preaching, for we need to know more precisely how authentic this is /3/.

So far as the first of our questions is concerned, that concerning Isaiah's attitude to Hezekiah's joining the coalition which rebelled against Assyria in 705, the answer is clear and definitive. Isaiah condemned it firmly and decisively, and foretold that it would lead to ruination. This comes out most clearly in the prophet's bitter condemnation of the negotiations with Egypt which formed Hezekiah's main hope of support:

Isaiah and the Deliverance of Jerusalem

Woe to the rebellious children, says Yahweh,
who carry out a plan, but not mine;
and who make a league, but not of my spirit,
that they may add sin to sin;
who set out to go down to Egypt,
without asking for my counsel,
to take refuge in the protection of Pharaoh,
and to seek shelter in the shadow of Egypt.
Therefore shall the protection of Pharaoh turn to
your shame,
and the shelter in the shadow of Egypt to your
humiliation.
For though his officials are at Zoan and his envoys
reach Hanes,
every one comes to shame through a people that
cannot profit them,
that brings neither help nor profit,
but shame and disgrace.

(Isa. 30:1-5)

A precisely comparable message is to be found in Isa.
31:1-3, with an even clearer pronouncement that both Egypt
and Judah will come to ruin together:

Woe to those who go down to Egypt for help
and rely on horses,
who trust in chariots because they are many
and in horsemen because they are very strong,
but do not look to the Holy One of Israel or
consult Yahweh.
And yet he is wise and brings disaster,
he does not call back his words,
but will arise against the house of the evildoers,
and against the helpers of those who work
iniquity.
The Egyptians are men, and not God;
and their horses are flesh, and not spirit.
When Yahweh stretches out his hand,
the helper will stumble, and he who is helped will fall,
and they will all perish together.

(Isa. 31:1-3)

The message is perfectly clear, and it cannot be said that it
is to be understood simply as a rejection by the prophet of a

Two: The Threat to Jerusalem

treaty alliance with a foreign power on the grounds that all such alliances are signs of a want of faith in God. This is undoubtedly a major theme with the prophet, but, however we explain the theology that lies behind it, it is incontestable that the prophet affirmed here that the end result of this particular treaty would be disaster for both Judah and Egypt. There are certainly other passages in the book of Isaiah which express a similar theme, and several of these almost certainly belong to the period of the years 705-701, which was marked by Hezekiah's rebellion. (Cf. Isa. 28:14-22; 30:6-7, 8-17. Isa. 18:1-6 and 19:1-5 may also belong to this period, but are more probably to be assigned to the earlier time of the Ashdodite rebellion (713-711), which Hezekiah was strongly pressed to join, and where Egyptian military aid was promised.)

In the light of this clear condemnation of Hezekiah's plan to rebel against Assyria we can go further and deduce that some of the warnings given by Isaiah regarding an attack by an alien army upon Jerusalem also belong to this period. The clearest example here is Isa. 29:1-4:

Ho, Ariel, Ariel,
    the city where David encamped!
Add year to year;
    let the feasts run their round.
Yet I will distress Ariel,
    and there shall be moaning and lamentation,
    and she shall be to me like an Ariel.
And I will encamp against you round about,
    and will besiege you with towers
    and I will raise siegeworks against you.
Then deep from the earth you shall speak,
    from low in the dust your words shall come;
your voice shall come from the ground like the voice
        of a ghost,
    and your speech shall whisper out of the dust.
                        (Isa. 29:1-4)

Isa. 31:4 should almost certainly be located at the same time, that of the threat to Jerusalem from the army of Sennacherib:

For thus Yahweh said to me,
As a lion or a young lion growls over his prey,

31

and when a band of shepherds is called forth against him
he is not terrified by their shouting
or daunted at their noise,
So Yahweh of hosts will come down
to fight against mount Zion and against its hill.
(Isa. 31:4)

It is important in regard to this key verse to recognize that God's action is to be directed <u>against</u> Jerusalem and Mount Zion, and that he is not simply to come "upon" (Heb. 'al) this place /4/. Yahweh is pictured as a lion who has seized his prey, so that the efforts of those who try to thwart him will be in vain. However much noise they make in an effort to frighten the lion into letting go of its prey they will not succeed.

It is possible that the portrayal of a hostile advance against Jerusalem now contained in Isa. 10:27b-32 also belongs to the year 701, but this is far from certain, and this difficult passage can more convincingly be placed earlier, perhaps in the years 713-711 /5/. Certainly the difficulties which it raises preclude its being used to provide evidence to show how Isaiah envisaged the final outcome of the threat to Jerusalem posed by Sennacherib in 701. Similarly it is possible that other prophecies which threaten Jerusalem with military attack and defeat (e.g. Isa. 1:21-26 and 3:1-8) should also be ascribed to this time. More probably, however, they belong earlier, and were uttered by Isaiah during the later years of the reign of Ahaz. What we have so far considered, however, is quite sufficient to demonstrate beyond doubt that Isaiah both condemned the alliance between Judah and Egypt, which formed a major political platform upon which Hezekiah's rebellion against Assyria was based in the years 705-701, and foretold that disastrous consequences would come from it. That these consequences would be the work of God, who is portrayed as the enemy who would attack Jerusalem, is entirely in conformity with a well established prophetic convention (cf. Amos 7:8-9; Hos. 1:4 etc.). In reality Isaiah was fully aware that the enemy would be a human army, and there is no reason to doubt that he fully expected this to be the army of Assyria. God would act in this case, as he normally did, through his human agents (cf. Isa. 10:5).

So far we have obtained a consistent picture of Isaiah's preaching concerning Hezekiah's rebellion which gives no hint

Two: The Threat to Jerusalem

that he might, at the vital moment when the city of Jerusalem was directly threatened by the encircling Assyrian forces, have changed his attitude. Nor is there any plausible way by which we might explain that the prophet had in some strange way maintained contradictory attitudes in relation to the same event. There is no reason therefore why we should suppose that Isaiah first threatened Hezekiah, but then coupled this with a threat against the Assyrians who were advancing against Jerusalem /6/. We must assume that he remained consistent in his attitude, so that the only way in which we could find room for a warning of the impending destruction of the Assyrian armies which were attacking Jerusalem would be to argue that, at some point, he turned sharply against them, after initially regarding them as having fulfilled the chastisement upon Judah determined by God. This has been the attraction of the supposition that a second siege of Jerusalem took place later in 701, since it would allow that the prophet might have been incensed at what he, and the citizens of Jerusalem, took to be a betrayal of an oath sworn by the Assyrians in accepting the surrender of Hezekiah /7/.

Yet such a hypothesis regarding a second siege of Jerusalem in the year 701 is in itself improbable, and must be ruled out on the evidence to be found in certain other prophecies from Isaiah. The most important of these is to be found in Isa. 22:1-4 and emanates from the time immediately after Hezekiah's surrender to Sennacherib and the lifting of the threatened siege of Jerusalem. The original Isaianic prophecy has been expanded by editorial additions and interpretations in 22:5-8a and 8b-11. These were almost certainly made very soon after the destruction of Jerusalem by the Babylonian armies in 587 B.C. /8/. Very probably vv.12-14 are also originally from Isaiah, as the majority of critical commentators have concluded, but whether they formed the original continuation of vv.1-4, as most have believed, seems less certain. In any case the fact that Isaiah's prophecy in Isa. 22:1-4, which so severely castigates the citizens of Jerusalem for their behaviour after the deliverance of the city in 701, was added to after 587 is of quite special interest:

What do you mean that you have gone up,
    all of you to the housetops,

you who are full of shoutings,
   tumultous city, exultant town?
Your slain are not slain with the sword
   or dead in battle.
All your rulers have fled together,
   without the bow they were captured.
All of you who were found were captured,
   though they had fled far away.
Therefore I said:
   Look away from me,
let me weep bitter tears;
do not labour to comfort me
   for the destruction of the daughter of my people.
                            (Isa. 22:1-4)

It is very clear from this passage that nothing at all is implied about a remarkable and unexpected defeat of the Assyrian army which had been facing Jerusalem. On the contrary Isaiah very openly regarded what had happened to Judah as the destruction of God's people. Hence any rejoicing on the part of the survivors in Jerusalem, which in human terms was natural and understandable enough, is condemned by the prophet as misplaced and a further act of sin. It would therefore bring down further judgement upon them in the future, a point which has been elaborated upon by the post-587 editors. It is entirely in keeping with Isaiah's previous pronouncements that he describes God as leading the attack upon his people on account of their sins. No word at all is said that Yahweh had also been forced at this time to act against the Assyrians. Contrarily such a view would have conflicted sharply with the basis of the prophet's rebuke. Isa. 22:12-14 may then once have formed the continuation of this prophecy, or, more plausibly, these verses may represent a parallel prophecy addressed to the same situation with essentially the same message.

We have a further portrayal in Isa. 1:4-8 of the situation of Jerusalem after the act of surrender by Hezekiah. The picture that it presents of Zion "left like a booth in a vineyard" could possibly be taken to apply to the situation of Jerusalem at the time of Sennacherib's advance upon the city, and before Hezekiah's submission. Yet we must rule out such a conclusion since, in line with 22:1-4, the rebuke implicit in the prophecy centres upon the fact that Jerusalem

Two: The Threat to Jerusalem

and Judah have suffered so much, and yet have learnt so little from these sufferings. As it now stands there is a concluding verse (v.9) which pictures Jerusalem's isolated position as a continuing one and which elicits some message of hope from the fact of the city's survival. This single verse has certainly been added, sometime after 587 B.C., to the original prophecy which was consistently threatening in tone. By this time the hope of a renewal of Israel after the Babylonian exile had begun to emerge /9/:

Ah, sinful nation,
    a people laden with iniquity,
    offspring of evildoers,
    sons who deal corruptly!
they have forsaken Yahweh,
    they have despised the Holy One of Israel,
    they are utterly estranged.
Why will you still be smitten,
    that you continue to rebel?
The whole head is sick,
    and the whole heart faint.
From the sole of the foot even to the head,
    there is no soundness in it,
but bruises and sores and bleeding wounds;
    they are not pressed out, or bound up,
    or softened with oil.
Your country lies desolate,
    your cities are burned with fire;
    in your very presence aliens devour your land;
    it is desolate as overthrown by aliens.
And the daughter of Zion is left
    like a booth in a vineyard,
like a lodge in a cucumber field,
    like a besieged city.
                    (Isa. 1:4-8)

Once again, as in the case of Isa. 22:1-4, we find that we have a prophecy from the year 701, which is confidently to be ascribed to Isaiah, but which offers no support at all to the belief that Jerusalem had been the scene of a quite unexpected defeat of the Assyrians. The prophecy is not in itself at all hopeful about the future of Jerusalem, and it is only the later addition of v.9 which has given to the unit the

35

suggestion that Jerusalem forms a favoured "remnant" of the people of Israel. The judgement that had been meted out to Judah had been a terrible punishment from Yahweh, and Jerusalem had been fully complicit in the guilt that had occasioned this.

In the light of this prophecy we have no difficulty at all in piecing together a completely coherent account of what had happened to Judah in the years 705-701, and of the attitude which Isaiah had adopted towards these events. When first the alliance with Egypt had been formulated Isaiah had condemned it for its false security, and had foretold that it would lead to disastrous consequences for both Judah and Egypt. As the politial situation had developed in which Sennacherib had advanced against Judah and Jerusalem, so Isaiah had, with complete consistency, warned that this was a judgement which Judah had deservedly brought upon itself. When the siege of Jerusalem became imminent, Isaiah had maintained that the city would fall, and could not now be rescued out of the hands of Sennacherib (so especially Isa. 31:4). After Hezekiah's surrender, which had averted any further bloodshed and the physical destruction of Jerusalem, Isaiah had rebuked the citizens of Jerusalem for their rejoicing over the escape. The picture that he painted of the situation which had come about was of a terrible judgement which had been threatened, and which had been inflicted in full measure. That Jerusalem had survived without massive physical destruction was not an event which could be viewed as a mark of a special act of deliverance, since the wider perspective showed so clearly that it had to be viewed in the context of the ruin of the entire land.

So far then we have found a quite satisfactory consistency in Isaiah's preaching during the years 705-701 B.C. At no time had he promised Hezekiah that he, or his city, would be the subject of a special protection by Yahweh from the grip of Sennacherib. There are, however, scattered throughout chapters 1-39 of the book of Isaiah a number of passages which give a very clear and decided declaration that a time would come when the Assyrians would be punished by Yahweh for their blasphemous pride in their own achievements. The most important of these prophecies is to be found in Isa. 10:5-15, although vv.10-11 and the prose v.12 are two separate glosses which have been added in expansion of the

Two: The Threat to Jerusalem

original prophecy. That this is from Isaiah himself must be regarded as beyond doubt, although it is very difficult to determine the period of Isaiah's ministry to which it belongs. Almost certainly it was delivered after the fall of Samaria in 722 B.C., since the character of Assyrian domination is fully presupposed. Very probably also the prophecy evidences a familiarity with the character and content of certain Assyrian victory inscriptions. Yet at the same time it becomes clear from its message that it affirms the certainty, rather than the imminence, of Yahweh's punishment of the Assyrians. There is nothing in what it affirms therefore to suggest that it is to be linked with the events of the years 705-701 B.C. Most probably we should relate it to the years 722-715 B.C., before the outbreak of the Ashdodite rebellion against Assyria. Its purpose is unmistakably plain: to condemn the Assyrians for their arrogant pride and boasting and to affirm that a time would come when they too would be punished by Yahweh. When this would come and what form it would take are not explicitly spelt out:

Ah, Assyria, the rod of my anger,
   the staff of my fury!
Against a godless nation I send him,
   and against the people of my wrath I command him,
   to take spoil and seize plunder,
   and to tread them down like the mire of the streets.
But he does not so intend,
   and his mind does not so think;
but it is in his mind to destroy,
   and to cut off nations not a few;
for he says:
Are not my commanders all kings?
   Is not Calno like Carchemish?
   Is not Samaria like Damascus?
By the strength of my hand I have done it,
   and by my wisdom, for I have understanding;
I have removed the boundaries of peoples,
   and have plundered their treasures;
   like a bull I have brought down those who sat
     on thrones.
My hand has found like a nest the wealth of the peoples;
   and as men gather eggs that have been forsaken
   so I have gathered all the earth;

and there was none that moved a wing,
 or opened the mouth, or chirped.
Shall the axe vaunt itself over him who hews with it,
 or the saw magnify itself against him who wields it?
As if a rod should wield him who lifts it,
 or as if a staff should lift him who is not wood!
(Isa. 10:5-9, 13-15)

The prophecy is in the form of a disputation oracle, affirming that God was using Assyria as a rod with which to chastise his people, but that the king of Assyria believed himself to be acting in his own interest and by his own power. By pressing the analogy the prophet shows that the Assyrian king had no power other than that which had been given to him by God, so that his own boastful claims were an act of blasphemy. It is this element which suggests very positively that the prophet was familiar with the character and content of Assyrian victory inscriptions. By defining the offence so as to show that a blasphemy had been expressed Isaiah gives a firm implication that the Assyrian king would be punished for this sinful arrogance. However no clear pronouncement is included to show how, or when, this would take place. We find that some indication has been added later in vv.16-19, but these verses cannot have formed a part of the original prophecy. No indication of the date of the original prophecy is given, and the editor who added v.12 has simply sought to make clear that the punishment of the Assyrians would take place at a time when Yahweh's work against Jerusalem had been "finished". Most probably we should locate the original Isaianic prophecy between the years 722 and 715 B.C., after the fall of Samaria, but before the first political moves which led to the Ashdodite rebellion, which we know Isaiah condemned (cf. Isa. 20). In its essential content there is nothing in this important prophecy to link it with any direct political uprising against the Assyrians which could suggest that Isaiah envisaged a particular military action as the occasion when the king of Assyria would be punished by Yahweh. There are no clear grounds therefore for thinking that this was a prophecy which related to the threatened siege of Jerusalem by Sennacherib in 701 B.C. We do not need to doubt the Isaianic origin of the prophecy therefore, but with equal certainty we cannot find in it any evidence at all to suggest that Isaiah had expected the year 701 to provide a spectacular setback, or defeat, for the military might of Assyria.

We can find in the prophecy of Isa. 10:5-15* a foundation for the belief that Isaiah had foretold that a time would come when the king of Assyria would be defeated and punished, but not that Isaiah connected this in any way with the time or circumstances of Hezekiah's revolt against Sennacherib, which we know Isaiah condemned. We must now turn to consider another prophecy of unique significance, not because it explicitly threatened the overthrow of Assyria, but because of its strong note of assurance regarding the future greatness of Israel under a Davidic ruler. This is to be found in Isa. 9:2-7 (Heb. 9:1-6), and the question of its authenticity to Isaiah has been much more vigorously disputed. We need not enter into the many points of critical discussion, which I have dealt with more fully in my commentary, but may set out the following salient conclusions:

1. Verse 9:1 (Heb. 8:23) was not a part of the original prophecy, but has been introduced quite early as a note defining the historical circumstances against which the ensuing hopeful prophecy is to be understood. As such it must be understood in a consistently negative fashion of the destruction wrought by the Assyrians upon Israel. It does not therefore reflect the more hopeful situation which emerged during Josiah's reign, as H. Barth and others have argued /10/.

2. The prophecy of 9:2-7 is then to be understood as an accession oracle for a new king (of the Davidic line), modelled upon the formal court oracles of this kind.

3. This new Davidic king must have been Hezekiah, and the date of his accession we may set sometime in 725 B.C. The basic prophecy is addressed to all Israel, comprising both Ephraim and Judah, although part of the intention of the addition of the note in 9:1 is to show that it was especially addressed to Ephraim, which the editor regarded as now lost to Assyria.

4. The purpose of this royal prophecy, which has acquired a uniquely "messianic" character during the history of its interpretation, was originally to set out the terms by which, as the prophet understood them, Israel's salvation was to be achieved. Its intention therefore was not to suggest that the age of salvation and the overthrow of Assyria were now imminent events, but rather to show the way by which the

wounds of the past could be healed, and Israel's former greatness recovered.

With these considerations in mind nothing stands in the way of finding in the prophecy a genuine utterance from Isaiah, given at the time when Ahaz's death had removed one obstacle to Israel's renewal of obedience to Yahweh and when the traditional hopes associated with kingship were given fresh meaning:

> The people who walked in darkness have seen a
> > great light;
> those who dwell in a land of deep darkness,
> > on them has light shined.
> Thou hast multiplied the nation,
> > thou hast increased its joy;
> they rejoice before thee
> > as with joy at the harvest,
> > as men rejoice when they divide the spoil.
> For the yoke of his burden,
> > and the staff for his shoulder,
> > the rod of his oppressor,
> > thou hast broken as on the day of Midian.
> For every boot of the tramping warrior in battle tumult
> > and every garment rolled in blood
> > will be burned as fuel for the fire.
> For unto us a child is born,
> > to us a son is given;
> and the government will be upon his shoulder,
> > and his name will be called
> "Wonderful Counsellor, Mighty God,
> > Everlasting Father, Prince of Peace."
> Of the increase of his government and of peace
> > there will be no end,
> upon the throne of David, and over his kingdom,
> > to establish it, and to uphold it
> with justice and righteousness
> > from this time forth and for evermore.
> The zeal of Yahweh of hosts will do this.
>
> > (Isa. 9:2-7 [Heb. 1-6])

The theme of the prophecy is the salvation which Israel is to enjoy under a Davidic ruler, and, if the setting that we have adopted for it in accordance with the suggestion

Two: The Threat to Jerusalem

originally proposed by A. Alt /11/ is sound, then it can be given a firm date in Isaiah's ministry. The "birth" of v.6 must be understood as an image of royal accession (cf. Ps. 2:7).Its broad theme of promise, and of Israel's coming greatness, does not link it directly to any specific military threat against Assyria. Accordingly we must rule out any idea that this prophecy provided Hezekiah with any encouragement to rebel, either in the period 713-711, or in that of 705-701. Still less can we relate it directly to the events of 701 in such a fashion as to suggest that Isaiah deliberately drew upon the reassuring features of the Davidic-Zion tradition at the time when Jerusalem was directly threatened by the armies of Sennacherib. The political situation to which the prophecy was addressed was that of Hezekiah's accession, with its attendant possibilities, not an imminent confrontation between Hezekiah and Sennacherib.

We must turn now to consider a number of passages which are scattered throughout chapters 1-39 of the book of Isaiah, and which many commentators have linked directly with Isaiah's preaching at the time of the Assyrian crisis of 701. The question of their authenticity to Isaiah, and the general dependence which they have been thought to reveal upon the so-called "Zion tradition", may be dealt with when we have looked at them in more detail. It is sufficient at this stage simply to note that it is these passages, or at least certain of them, which have frequently been adduced by commentators and exegetes in an endeavour to show that Isaiah had explicitly prophesied that the army of Sennacherib would suffer a dramatic reversal outside the very gates of Jerusalem. These passages are to be found in 10:16-19, 33f.; 14:24-27; 17:12-14; 29:5-8; 31:5, 8f. In recent years the supposition of Isaiah's strong dependence upon the Zion motif of the Jerusalem cult has led to the further linking of 8:9f. with these verses.

Already in 1888 S.R. Driver argued that the two prophecies now preserved in 14:24-27 and 17:12-14 were delivered by Isaiah in reassurance to Hezekiah at the time of the threat from Sennacherib in 701 B.C. /12/. Even more emphatically in recent years, such exegetes as G. von Rad and J. Schreiner have sought to find in such passages evidence both of Isaiah's dependence upon a central theme of Zion's inviolability which was supposedly transmitted in the Jerusalem cultus, and of

41

his attitude to the threat from Sennacherib /13/.

We may deal with the passages in the order in which they appear in the book, although it is necessary to bear in mind that not all interpreters have regarded them all as relating to the situation of Sennacherib's assault upon Judah in 701. The first of them is to be found in 10:16-19, and appears as an immediate sequel to the important Isaianic prophecy of 10:5-15* which we have already considered:

> Therefore Yahweh, Yahweh of hosts,
>   will send wasting sickness among his stout warriors,
> and under his glory a burning will be kindled,
>   like the burning of fire.
> The light of Israel will become a fire,
>   and his Holy One a flame;
> and it will burn and devour
>   his thorn and briers in one day.
> The glory of his forest and of his fruitful land,
>   Yahweh will destroy, both soul and body,
>   and it will be as when a sick man wastes away.
> The remnant of the trees of his forest will be so few
>   that a child can write them down.
>   (Isa. 10:16-19)

The secondary nature of the prophecy, and with this the certain deduction that it does not derive from Isaiah himself but from later editors, is shown as soon as we note its dependence on genuine Isaianic prophecies. Most strikingly is this apparent in regard to the reference to the "thorns and briers" in v.17, which derives from the imagery of the Song of the Vineyard of Isa. 5:1-7 (so v.6). The application of this imagery here, however, refers it to the Assyrian army, so that it has almost certainly been employed in its present context by way of its secondary application in Isa. 7:24 to men "with bows and arrows". In this latter instance it is found alongside two other interpretations of the threat of the coming of "thorns and briers". This alone may suffice to demonstrate the secondary character of Isa. 10:16-19, but such a conclusion is reinforced by the fact that we have a further similar development. The "light of Israel" referred to in v.17, which is to become a fire, has been taken from the promise of the appearance of a "great light" given in 9:2. Once this distinctive character of v.17 has been recognized,

it becomes probable that the whole of the unit comprised of
vv.16-19 has arisen in a similar fashion by a kind of midrashic
exegesis of authentic Isaianic sayings /14/. In fact the
metaphor of Assyria as a great forest (v.18), for there can be
little doubt that it is Assyria that is being referred to, has
most probably been developed from the image of the "rod" of
Isa. 10:5, and the general application of woodcutting in the
same prophecy in 10:15.

We can therefore dismiss the possibility that Isa. 10:16-19
comes from Isaiah in the eighth century. However, since it
fully recognizes that Assyria is still an enemy to Israel, and
since it appears still to regard the final overthrow of the
Assyrian imperial power as in the future, it cannot have
arisen later than the end of the seventh century. It is
therefore almost certainly to be ascribed to the period of
Josiah's reign in the latter half of the seventh century and
must have formed a part of the extensive anti-Assyrian
redaction made to Isaiah's prophecies at that time /15/.

The "prophecy" in reality consists of a kind of "midrashic"
elaboration of images drawn from authentic sayings from
Isaiah, most especially the prophecies of 5:1-7; 9:1-6 and
10:5-15*. In essence it represents a carrying-forward of
Isaiah's warning that a time of punishment would come for
the Assyrians, and has arisen at a period in Josiah's reign
when the downfall of Assyria appeared at last as a political
and military possibility. There is no reason to suppose that
the editors who have composed it intended it to refer to what
had happened in 701. It is not in essence a new prophecy at
all, but rather a re-affirmation of the quite authentic warning by Isaiah that Assyria would be punished for its blasphemous arrogance.

The prophecy of 10:33f. is very similar in character and
represents a further elaboration of the image of Assyria as a
forest, which is to be cut down:

Behold, Yahweh, Yahweh of hosts,
    will lop the boughs with terrifying power;
the great in height will be hewn down,
    and the lofty will be brought low.
He will cut down the thickets of the forest with an axe,
    and Lebanon with its majestic trees will fall.
                (Isa. 10:33f.)

These two verses cannot have formed the original continuation of Isa. 10:27b-32, which we have taken to be an authentic Isaianic saying. We can, without great difficulty, see that a quite clear redactional stucture has been imposed on the entire section of Isa. 10:5-34. The two basic Isaiah prophecies dealing with Assyria are to be found in 10:5-15* and vv.27b-32. To each of these a threat elaborating upon the theme of the punishment of Assyria, and centering upon the image of Assyria as a "forest", has been appended in vv.16-19 and 33-34. These redactional additions must have been made during Josiah's reign when Assyrian power in Judah was waning, but when the final overthrow of that power had still not taken place. The intervening two sections in vv.20-23, which elaborate upon the theme of the "remnant" from Isa. 7:3, and vv.24-27, which build upon the image of the breaking of the rod of the oppressor from 9:4, must similarly derive from the time of the Josianic redaction of Isaiah's prophecies. H. Barth would place these two sections rather later /16/, but this appears both unnecessary and improbable, especially in view of the fact that after the death of Josiah the Assyrian threat had effectively ceased to exist for Judah. The "remnant" imagery of 10:20-23 is concerned with the remnant of the Northern Kingdom of Ephraim, and is elaborated from different interpretations of the significance of the name of Isaiah's son, Shear-jashub. The exhortation of vv.24-27 then summarises very conveniently the message that is offered to Judah and Israel in consequence of the divine assurance that the days of Assyrian rule will shortly be brought to an end. In fact these verses present with stark simplicity the major theme of the entire Josianic edition of Isaiah's prophecies:

> Therefore thus says Yahweh, Yahweh of hosts: "O my people, who dwell in Zion, be not afraid of the Assyrians when they smite with the rod and lift up their staff against you as the Egyptians did. For in a very little while my indignation will come to end, and my anger will be directed to their destruction. And Yahweh of hosts will wield against them a scourge, as when he smote Midian at the rock of Oreb; and his rod will be over the sea, and he will lift it as he did in Egypt. And in that day his burden will depart from your neck."
> (Isa. 10:24-27)

Two: The Threat to Jerusalem

The direct literal citation of the words and assurance of 9:4 shows the same "midrashic" technique that we have already noted, and there can be little reason to doubt that it is the actual Assyrian power that is meant, not a later Mesopotamian power such as that of Babylon. The overthrow of this great imperial power is felt to be imminent and assured, and the basis for this assurance is found in Isaiah's prophecy of the new Davidic ruler, Isa. 9:2-7. The use of this prophecy in this fashion provides, incidentally, a quite strong and unexpected support for the claim to its Isaianic authenticity.

In the next of the passages which proclaim the dramatic overthrow of the Assyrians we encounter a saying which has been in the very forefront of the arguments that Isaiah did promise that Sennacherib's army would be defeated outside Jerusalem. This is to be found in Isa. 14:24-27:

> Yahweh of hosts has sworn:
> "As I have planned so shall it be,
> and as I have purposed so shall it stand,
> that I will break the Assyrian in my land,
> and upon my mountains trample him under foot;
> and his yoke shall depart from them,
> and his burden from their shoulder."
> This is the purpose that is purposed
> concerning the whole earth;
> and this is the hand that is stretched out
> over all the nations.
> For Yahweh of hosts has purposed,
> and who will annul it?
> His hand is stretched out,
> and who will turn it back?
>
> (Isa. 14:24-27)

Most striking here is the direct citation of 9:4 in verse 25, which has led several commentators to strike out v.25b as a gloss, since it is so self-evidently secondary. Yet in fact we must recognise that this is a false proceeding and that the entire unit is a secondary "midrashic" elaboration of Isaianic themes. The idea of Yahweh's special "plan" to destroy the Assyrians is dependant upon the concept of Yahweh's plan in 30:1, whilst the theme of the stretching out of Yahweh's hand has been taken from the refrain of 9:12, 17, 21; 5:25. The entire section is simply a further development of the belief that Isaiah had foretold that Yahweh would overthrow the Assyrians. It has been introduced into its present position to round off the important redactional unit of 5:1-14:27, which concerns the fate of Israel and Judah at the hands of the Assyrians.

We may now turn to the fourth of the passages which foretell the overthrow of Assyria, bearing in mind that so far we have found nothing which suggests that Isaiah had linked such an overthrow with the time, or circumstances, which prevailed in 701 B.C. This is to be found in Isa. 17:12-14:

> Ah, the thunder of many peoples,
> they thunder like the thundering of the sea!
> Ah, the roar of the nations,
> they roar like the roaring of mighty waters!
> The nations roar like the roaring of many waters,
> but he will rebuke them, and they will flee far away,
> chased like chaff on the mountains before the wind
> and whirling dust before the storm.
> At evening time, behold, terror!
> Before morning, they are no more!
> This is the portion of those who despoil us,
> and the lot of those who plunder us.
>
> (Isa. 17:12-14)

The comparison of the noise of the attacking Assyrians with the roaring of the sea would appear to have been drawn from Isaiah's portrayal of their attack against Judah in 5:26-30, where it is specifically likened to the roaring of the sea (Isa. 5:30). Possibly also 8:7, with its metaphor of Assyria as "a mighty river", has further strengthened the use of this distinctive imagery for them and their overthrow. In any case the common subject matter relates the passage to those others which we have already noted. It announces the coming downfall of Assyria, but introduces nothing which suggests that this had taken place in the year 701 B.C. Rather this downfall was an event still in the future, even from the point of view of the Josianic redactors who have built up this assurance on the basis of Isaiah's prophecies. This particular passage may be taken to be of special interest on account of its great stress on the suddenness with which the power of Assyria will be thwarted, without giving any indication how this will be brought about. Taken together the two passages,

Two: The Threat to Jerusalem

Isa. 14:24-27 and 17:12-14, have frequently been thought to provide the strongest evidence that Isaiah foretold a defeat for Sennacherib in the year 701, and have been thought to show that Isaiah had been deeply influenced by a belief in Jerusalem's inviolability associated with the supposed "Zion tradition". In reality they show nothing of the kind, but are a part of a redactional elaboration of the assurance of the coming overthrow of Assyria, which had a quite authentic place in Isaiah's preaching.

The next passage that falls to be considered is found in Isa. 29:5-8, and this has clearly been placed in its present position in order to serve as an expansion, and corrective, to the threatening declaration of Yahweh's impending attack on Jerusalem in 29:1-4. This original Isaianic prophecy must belong to the year 701, and reflects Isaiah's sharp hostility towards Hezekiah's policy of rebellion and declares a frightful outcome to the forthcoming Assyrian attack on Jerusalem. The expansion falls into two separate parts, suggesting that it may even have been formulated in two stages. The first part, in vv.5-6, announces the overthrow of Judah's foes, and the second part, in vv.7-8, gives a broader application of this to "all the nations":

But the multitude of your foes shall be like small dust,
    and the multitude of the ruthless like passing chaff.
And in an instant, suddenly,
    you will be visited by Yahweh of hosts
with thunder and earthquake and great noise,
    with whirlwind and tempest, and the flame
        of a devouring fire.
And the multitude of all the nations that fight
        against Ariel,
    all that fight against her and her stronghold
        and distress her,
    shall be like a dream, a vision of the night.
As when a hungry man dreams he is eating
    and awakes with his hunger not satisfied,
or as when a thirsty man dreams he is drinking
    and awakes faint, with his thirst not quenched,
so shall the multitide of all the nations be
    that fight against Mount Zion.
                                            (Isa. 29:5-8)

Isaiah and the Deliverance of Jerusalem

The comparison between the coming destruction of the Assyrians and the blowing of chaff and dust in the wind is also to be found in 17:13. What we are presented with here is a further elaboration of the message that the Assyrians will be shattered by Yahweh. Like Isa. 17:12-14 it must derive from the redactors of Josiah's reign. All the traditional instruments of divine wrath - thunder, earthquake, whirlwind, tempest and lightning - are to be employed against the "foes" of Judah, but there can be no doubt that it is the Assyrians who are primarily being referred to. What is interesting in this further elaboration of Isaiah's message of the overthrow of the Assyrians, is that its redactional position may provide us with a pointer to show how the belief began to emerge that such an act of divine wrath had been inflicted on the Assyrians in 701. Since the original prophecy of Isa. 29:1-4 belongs to that year, it is understandable that the assumption came to be made that the ensuing verses, 5-8, also related to events of that year, although this is quite evidently not what was originally intended in the Josianic redaction of Isaiah's prophecies.

The last of the passages which especially concern us on account of their declaration of a sudden divine defeat to be inflicted on the Assyrian attackers of Judah is to be found in 31:5, 8-9. Again this time the section falls into two parts, the first affirming Yahweh's intention to protect Jerusalem (Isa. 31:5), and the second (vv.8-9), announcing the coming destruction of the Assyrians by the hand of God. This probably indicates that the section has grown up in two stages, although the intervening two verses (Isa. 31:6-7) contain two appeals to the people of Israel to turn back to Yahweh and to repudiate all use of images. Undoubtedly these verses are a yet later editorial addition, designed to elicit a more timelessly applicable message from what Yahweh had done for Jerusalem. There can be little reason for questioning that the verses announcing the special protection afforded to Jerusalem and the consequent defeat of Assyria derive, like the others we have been considering, from the Josianic elaboration of Isaiah's prophecies. We may take the two parts separately:

Like birds hovering, so Yahweh of hosts
will protect Jerusalem;

he will protect and deliver it,
    he will spare and rescue it.
                                    (Isa. 31:5)

This verse is a particularly striking example of the method of exegetical elaboration of Isaiah's prophecies which we have seen to be characteristic of the Josianic redactors. The image of a large bird hovering to protect its nest comes strangely unanticipated, and appears rather inappropriate after the preceding image of the lion's refusal to be daunted by advancing shepherds in an effort to make it release its prey. Yet the new image immediately makes sense once it is related to the image of the bird's nest which occurs in the central prophecy of 10:5-15*:

My hand has found like a nest
    the wealth of the peoples;
and as men gather eggs that have been forsaken
    so I have gathered all the earth;
and there was none that moved a wing,
    or opened a mouth, or chirped.
                                    (Isa. 10:14)

The "prophecy" that follows on from 31:5 and announces the fall of Assyria by the hand of God is significant especially because of its clear declaration that this event will not be brought about by ordinary military action:

"And the Assyrian shall fall by a sword, not of man;
    and a sword, not of man, shall devour him;
and he shall flee from the sword,
    and his young men shall be put to forced labour.
His rock shall pass away in terror,
    and his officers desert the standard in panic,"
says Yahweh, whose fire is in Zion,
    and whose furnace is in Jerusalem.
                                    (Isa. 31:8-9)

It is not explicitly affirmed that the destruction of the Assyrians (vv.8-9), and their consequent enslavement, was to take place contemporaneously with the special divine protection which Yahweh would extend over Jerusalem (v.5), although this might later have been inferred. What we are presented with in this, as in the other related passages, is a straightforward redactional elaboration of the Isaianic

49

message that Yahweh would eventually overthrow the Assyrians (Isa. 10:5-15*). The manner of this editorial development has, however, led to a number of interesting innovations. First of all, it has introduced the idea that it would be linked to a special providential act of protection for Jerusalem, and this is quite clearly a <u>de facto</u> inference made in the wake of the events of 701. More strikingly, however, Isaiah's conventional use of the prophetic idiom that it would be the hand of Yahweh that was lifted against Assyria has given rise to a unique emphasis upon the direct action of God in this punitive overthrow. Overall the perspective that is presented is one of a divine act of punishment that was still in the future, not only from the standpoint of Isaiah's time, but also from that of the Josianic redactors. Yet it was the expected imminence of this overthrow under the reign of Josiah, and with it the ending of the century-long nightmare of Assyrian imperial domination, that has occasioned the very distinctive extension of Isaiah's prophecy. In the content of what is affirmed, both in Isaiah's original prophecy in 10:5-15*, and in the subsequent redactional development of this with the aid of other themes and images taken from Isaiah's prophecies, there is nothing to suggest that Isaiah himself had expected a sudden overthrow of the Assyrian army to be inflicted upon it in the year 701, nor, in retrospect, was this thought to have occurred. What happened then was that Jerusalem was providentially spared, and only the juxtaposition of Isa. 29:5-8 with 29:1-4, and of 31:5, 8-9 with 31:1-4, might later have led to the false inference that the events of the year 701 witnessed the fulfilment of Isaiah's threat to the power of the Assyrian king. In reality the very content of the Josianic redactional elaboration of Isaiah's message regarding the Assyrians shows that their overthrow was still not thought to have taken place by Josiah's reign. Prophecy marched in step with history, so that the special concern during that king's reign with what Isaiah had declared to be the ultimate fate of the power of Assyria arose because it was in Josiah's time that the political situation made its fulfilment possible.

So far as the content of the Isaiah narrative of 2 Kings 18:13-19:37 is concerned, we have succeeded in clarifying a number of major points. Isaiah not only condemned Hezekiah's act of rebellion against Assyria, but foretold that its outcome would be disastrous for both Judah and Egypt. The promise of military assistance from Egypt was worthless. At no point did Isaiah mitigate the sharpness of this threat, nor did he revoke it. Even after Hezekiah's early surrender had spared Jerusalem the horrors of military conflict, Isaiah refused to allow the citizens of that city to indulge in any self-congratulatory celebrations, and insisted that what had happened had been a disaster. His message that a time would come when the Assyrians would be overthrown "by the hand of Yahweh" was never related by him, or his Josianic editors, to the events of the year 701. At the most there was a softening of tone in the work of the Josianic editors to regard the fact that Jerusalem had not fallen in battle in that year as a mark of special divine protection (cf. Isa. 31:5). We must conclude therefore that there is no justification at all for arguing that Isaiah had foretold the miraculous defeat of Sennacherib's assault on Jerusalem in 701 B.C. Those passages in the book of Isaiah which have been thought to support such a contention are not authentic to Isaiah, but are the work of redactors working in Josiah's reign. Even more pertinently, however, these passages were never intended to be addressed, even retrospectively, to the events that had taken place in 701 B.C. They merely reaffirm, from the vantage point of the weakening of Assyrian control of Judah in Josiah's reign, that the final overthrow of that power which Isaiah had announced was now imminent.

Chapter 3

THE ISAIAH NARRATIVES

The books of 1 and 2 Kings are rather puzzling to the student of the history of Israel's religion for their seemingly inconsistent attitude with regard to the prophets. On the one hand they regard prophecy as a major gift of God to his people and a paramount factor in his providential activity in history. Yet on the other they tell us virtually nothing of the work of the great prophets who were active during the period, the history of which they recount. Hence they do not explicitly mention Amos, Hosea, Micah or Jeremiah, whose sayings are recorded in the books of the Latter Prophets. The one great exception to this is Isaiah, who figures prominently in the major account of the deliverance of Jerusalem in 701 B.C. which forms the focal point of our next subject of attention. In fact the three stories which make up the trilogy of incidents recorded in 2 Kings 18:17-20:19 are frequently referred to as the "Isaiah narratives", because the prophet figures in each of them. Yet they are not stories about Isaiah as such, since his role is simply to proclaim the message of God relating to the incidents which are the main point of interest. However the three stories certainly belong together, and it becomes clear when we examine them that they are all, in rather different ways, concerned with the event of Jerusalem's deliverance from Sennacherib in 701, although this appears in only a brief note in the second of the stories (2 Kings 20:6) /1/. In fact the three stories are concerned with the role of Jerusalem and the Davidic kingship in God's purpose for Israel, for which the report of what happened in 701 provides the point of primary interest. We can then see that the other two incidents are narrated in order to bring out certain features which were felt to belong to a proper understanding of the primary event. Certainly the three stories belong together, although there are indications that they were not all composed at the same time, and that they have in fact been fashioned by a process of building up around a central theme. It appears most likely that they have been incorporated as a connected trilogy into the history of 2 Kings where they are now to be found.

Our next major task then must be to examine in detail, regarding both its literary structure and historical content, the narrative of 2 Kings 18:17-19:37, which, we have earlier pointed out, has come to be referred to critically as account B, to distinguish it from account A which is to be found in 2 Kings 18:13-16. In pursuing this examination we cannot but bear in mind that it is this narrative, telling of Jerusalem's miraculous escape from Sennacherib, which has occasioned the belief that a historical problem exists regarding this event, since the contents of this account B have frequently been felt to be irreconcilable with the information about the events of 701 which our other sources provide. Furthermore, in studying the passages in the book of Isaiah which have frequently been adduced in support of the claim that this prophet gave categorical assurance of the city's protection from the Assyrians we have found that these passages are secondary. They have been composed by a process of "midrashic" elaboration of Isaianic prophecies. They can be placed with reasonable confidence in the period of Josiah's reign when their message of a divine victory over the Assyrians had taken on a new significance. They are therefore "Isaianic" only in a rather extended sense. In view of the fact that we have already had occasion to note that our account B was composed some time after the event which forms its centrepiece had taken place, we already have some grounds for thinking that it may also belong to this same period of Josiah's reign. However this is a point which we must consider after examining the account, and which we cannot, at this stage, take for granted.

Since this account has been very fully and critically examined by B.S. Childs in relatively recent years, and since I am largely in agreement with his main literary conclusions, there is little need to reconsider many of the details of his analysis /2/. In any case these conclusions are themselves developed from a long tradition of scholarship stemming from observations made by B. Stade in 1886 /3/. This scholar noted that we have here not one account of what happened between Hezekiah and Sennacherib, but two. These two accounts run closely parallel with each other, and appear to represent variant recensions of the story following a closely similar theme and plot, although they have been combined together to make them run in sequence. There is, as a result, an awkward sense of duplication in the way in which the story of the negotiations is recounted /4/.

With the relatively minor modifications introduced by B.S. Childs, this leaves us with a B1 account in 2 Kings 18:17-19:9a + 36-37 and a B2 account in 2 Kings 19:9b-35. Both accounts follow a closely parallel plot and each of them raises a sharp accusation against Sennacherib for having blasphemed God by his arrogance in claiming his conquests as a mark of his own great power. The second account (B2) differs from the first by its inclusion of a lengthy citation of prophecies given by Isaiah, but most of all on account of its sudden and dramatic ending, which is unanticipated, and which has no counterpart in B1.

We may begin by considering the B1 account, which is the simpler of the two to deal with. It recounts how Sennacherib sent three emissaries from Lachish to Hezekiah in Jerusalem, and tells how the leader of these three, the Rabshakeh, made a bombastic speech to Hezekiah's three officials by the conduit of the upper pool on the highway to the Fuller's Field (2 Kings 18: 17-25). This speech refers to Hezekiah's religious reforms and to his confidence in his alliance with Egypt. The latter would appear to reflect a familiarity with Isaiah's preaching which sharply accused Hezekiah and his counsellors on account of their misplaced trust in Egypt (Isaiah 28:14ff.; 29:13ff; 30:1ff.; 31:1ff.). The mention of Hezekiah's reforms must be linked with the notice of these given in 2 Kings 18:3-6. After refusing a request to speak in Aramaic, the Rabshakeh is then said to have made a public speech in "the language of Judah" (2 Kings 18:28) elaborating upon his boasts concerning Hezekiah's inability to defend Jerusalem against Sennacherib, but warning that part of the price of submission would be wholesale deportation (v.32). The speech concludes with a challenging assertion that other gods have not been able to deliver their people out of the hand of the king of Assyria (2 Kings 18:28-35). The people and Hezekiah are duly intimidated until Isaiah gives a word of reassurance:

> Isaiah said to them, "Say to your master, 'Thus says Yahweh: Do not be afraid because of the words that you have heard, with which the servants of the king of

Three: The Isaiah Narratives

Assyria have reviled me. Behold I will put a spirit in him, so that he shall hear a rumour and return to his own land; and I will cause him to fall by the sword in his own land.'"
(2 Kings 19:6-7)

After decamping from Lachish to Libnah, the Assyrian king is then said to have heard a report concerning the movement of Tirhakah king of Ethiopia /5/. If we then accept that 2 Kings 19:36-7 forms the original conclusion of this B1 account, Sennacherib thereafter departed from Judah and returned to Nineveh where he was murdered. That a significant interval of time separated this assassination from the return is not specified, but is certainly not precluded /6/. The whole is clearly set out as a piece of narrative theology, closely echoing the language and ideas of Isaiah's prophecy in Isa. 10:5ff. The story requires no miraculous supernatural action on God's part, who simply causes Sennacherib to hear a report of a move by Tirhakah which compelled him to depart from Judah without pressing his attack upon Jerusalem. There is no mention of a siege of the city, and no reference is made to the payment of a huge and humiliating indemnity by Hezekiah. There is a historical problem regarding the accuracy and authenticity of the mention of the move by Tirhakah, but this could, without difficulty, be accounted for as the result of a slight confusion on the narrator's part and it does not seriously affect the main picture /7/. In itself there is nothing in the account which cannot be reconciled with the picture of events that is to be found in Sennacherib's annals and in account A /8/. For understandable reasons the theological interests of the Judean author have led him to omit to tell of the penalty suffered by Hezekiah, but neither has he given any indication that he regarded the incident as quite separate from an earlier confrontation between Sennacherib and Hezekiah. The account has obviously been written up at some time later than 701 as is shown by the mention of Sennacherib's death, which took place in 681. The two speeches of the Rabshakeh reveal themselves to be free compositions of the author since they have so evidently been included in order to bring out the theological implications of the Assyrian ruler's arrogance and pride of achievement. It is in fact the presence of these speeches which suggests a knowledge of Isaiah's prophecy of Isa. 10:5ff., where it is precisely this element of pride and self-exaltation over against God which the prophet has put into the mouth of the Assyrian king. Isaiah's role in the narrative is simply that of acting as God's mouthpiece in order to bring out the point that, by foretelling the event in advance, it will be evident that it is Yahweh who has thwarted Sennacherib of his purpose in conquering Jerusalem. It is worthy of particular note that the explanation that is provided of the way in which this will come about recognises that God works through human agencies, and in no way presupposes any directly supernatural action. If we had only this B1 account there would be very little serious difficulty in interpreting its contents as conformable to the picture that we have from elsewhere of Jerusalem's escape from any serious destruction in 701. What we are faced with is a story which has been strongly oriented in a particular theological manner, but which does not seriously depart from the facts of what happened in that important year. The fact that Jerusalem escaped ruination when virtually every other city and town of Judah experienced this has been elevated into a point of great theological significance.

It is when we come to consider the B2 account in 2 Kings 19:9b-35 that we encounter the greater difficulty in reconciling its contents with what we know from account A /8/. Yet we must bear in mind that the B2 account is widely recognised to be essentially a parallel variant of account B1. Hence it is in the points where B2 differs from B1 that the difficulty emerges most strongly in understanding its report as a further reference to the event of which we already have a full knowledge in accounts A and B1. The B2 story follows closely the theme and character of that of B1, save that the Assyrian king's boastful claims are sent to Hezekiah by a letter which he spreads out before God, who is the one who has been blasphemed by them. It especially points out that none of the gods of the peoples that Sennacherib had defeated previously had been able to save those who worshipped them. Hezekiah then offers a prayer to Yahweh, pointing out that it is his sovereignty that has been impugned. The prayer affirms that the God of Israel is the living God, whereas the gods of the defeated nations are not really gods, but have been made from wood and stone (2 Kings 19:15-19). The prayer brings out forcibly this particular feature of religious polemic, which is closely similar in language and substance to that which is to be found elsewhere in writings from the Deuteronomic school /9/. The answer from God is then said to have been sent by Isaiah to Hezekiah in a prophecy which is now quite extensive (2 Kings 19:21-34). However, on closer investigation, we find that this is in reality not one prophecy, but three. The first of these (vv.21-28) is addressed to the king of Assyria, accusing him of blasphemous arrogance and asserting:

> I will put my hook in your nose
>   and my bit in your mouth,
> and I will turn you back on the way
>   by which you came.
>
> (2 Kings 19:28)

The second prophecy is addressed to Hezekiah (vv.29-31) and is noteworthy because it displays an evidently secondary development of the theme of the remnant in vv.30 and 31 which has been derived from the prophecy of Isaiah concerning the name Shear-Jashub (Isa. 7:3; cf. Isa. 10:20-23 for comparable secondary developments of this theme). The third prophecy is to be found in vv.32-34, and is addressed openly to any hearer:

> Therefore thus says Yahweh concerning the king of Assyria, He shall not come into this city or shoot an arrow there, or come before it with a shield or cast up a siege mound against it. By the way that he came, by the same he shall return, and he shall not come into this city, says Yahweh. For I will defend this city to save it, for my own sake and for the sake of my servant David.
>
> (2 Kings 19:32-34)

This third prophecy is the most interesting of the three, as it is certainly also the most original of them in the B2 narrative. We may therefore agree with O. Kaiser that vv.21-31 have been interpolated, and are in fact dependent on the basic prophecy of vv.32-34 /10/. Very probably the interpolations about the remnant in vv.30-31 are the latest additions to have been made to this series of prophecies, all of which are ascribed to Isaiah. The third prophecy is the one therefore that we must consider in greatest detail because it holds the key to understanding the essential nature of the B2 account. It is formulated in the third person concerning "the

57

king of Assyria", suggesting that what is to happen to him is of interest to every reader. This is in line with the character of the account as a whole, which bears the form of a disputation narrative. The judgement that is pronounced upon the Assyrian king is clear: he will not lay siege to Jerusalem, and "By the way that he came, by the same he shall return" (v.33). The message is that he will go back to his own country without being able to fulfil his threats against Hezekiah and Jerusalem, exactly as in account B1. The reason why this will be so is then given in the form of an assertion that God will defend Jerusalem for his own sake and for the sake of his servant David. This adds a new feature to the theological significance of the account, and adds a further pointer to an understanding of the ideas which have moulded the general presentation. It implies that the reputation of the God of Israel was so closely allied to Jerusalem and its temple on account of the dynasty descending from David that he would not allow the city to suffer the fate that the Assyrians had inflicted on other nations. The story which then unfolds telling of the frustration of the plan of the king of Assyria to take Jerusalem serves as a demonstration that the God of Israel is the living God, whereas the gods of other nations are no gods at all.

The final climax of this B2 account then comes in v.35, which must in all respects be noted as the major problem verse with which we have to deal. It reads:

> And that night the angel of Yahweh went forth, and slew a hundred and eighty-five thousand in the camp of the Assyrians; and when men arose early in the morning, behold, these were all dead bodies.
>
> (2 Kings 19:35)

Were it not for this verse we should certainly have expected the conclusion of the B2 account to have followed closely that of B1, with the return of the king of Assyria to his homeland without his having destroyed Jerusalem. The prophecy which has been given points to such a conclusion, without even so much as mentioning how the divine will is to be carried out. Instead, in a strikingly miraculous dénouement of the story, the angel of Yahweh strikes down the Assyrian soldiers /11/. This is evidently not the conclusion to which the prophecy originally referred, since it is of a far more dramatic character, reducing the subsequent note of the king's return to the level of the commonplace, instead of being the point at which the prophecy is fulfilled. The mention of the return of Sennacherib to his homeland neither requires a previous act of destruction of his army, nor does it expect it. The most reasonable explanation for this, in the light of the literary evidence that we have, can only be that the B2 account once possessed an ending which ran closely parallel to that of B1. At the stage when the two accounts were combined together it became otiose, and was dropped. Instead there has come in, most probably at this time, but possibly after both accounts had already been combined, a verse which greatly heightens and exaggerates the manner in which God's purpose of thwarting Sennacherib was carried out. This one verse therefore, and with it the whole attempt to find some unique historical explanation of it through a plague or some other misfortune which befell the Assyrians, must be recognised for the late intrusion that it is. Without it, there is no serious difficulty in accepting that the B2 account, like that of B1, is a highly theologically motivated presentation of the event that we know took place in 701. It is true that there are minor points of conflict between the Old Testament accounts and the evidence from Sennacherib's Annals, but nothing sufficiently serious to require us to believe that the B account in 2 Kings 18:17-19:37 is referring to some other event than that described earlier in account A in 2 Kings 18:13-16. These discrepancies primarily concern the question whether or not a siege wall was set up around Jerusalem and whether the threat to Assyria from the Egyptians (Tirhakah) had materialised before the move against Jerusalem began /12/. Yet these are not major problems, once we allow that the B account has been written up after a considerable interval of time had elapsed, and is intended to draw the maximum in the way of theological significance out of the fact that Jerusalem was not subjected to any military attack. It is the single verse of 2 Kings 19:35 which gives rise to a more serious problem. Yet it is not at all difficult to suggest how this verse has arisen. We have ample evidence from our knowledge of what took place in 701 that Jerusalem's escape was due to Hezekiah's timely surrender, and not to any military encounter between the city's occupants and the Assyrians. The point that the deliverance would be an "act of God" has therefore become an important one in the development of the tradition about what happened. This is clearly to be seen in the content of the prophecy attributed to Isaiah in the B1 account (2 Kings 19:7) and in the prophecies formulated by Isaiah's redactors in Josiah's time relating to the destruction of the power of Assyria. As we have seen in the previous chapter, these characteristically employ a considerable element of hyperbole in affirming the divine power which will strike the Assyrians. We may note especially Isa. 31:8:

> And the Assyrian shall fall by a sword, not of man;
> and a sword, not of man, shall devour him;
> and he shall flee from the sword,
> and his young men shall be put to forced labour.
> (Isa. 31:8)

We may pause at this point to note also a most interesting verse which has been added secondarily to the collection of Hosea's prophecies, and which we may confidently ascribe to the period of the latter half of the seventh century B.C.:

> But I will have pity on the house of Judah, and I will deliver them by Yahweh their God; I will not deliver them by bow, nor by sword, nor by war, nor by horsemen.
> (Hos. 1:7 /13/)

The closeness of what is asserted here to the emphasis which we have found in the passages emanating from the Josianic redaction of Isaiah's prophecies points us unmistakeably to a recognition that the expectation of Yahweh's dramatic overthrow of the Assyrians was important in relation to other eighth century prophecies than those from Isaiah. For our present concern, however, it is the emphasis upon the divine power as the source of Jerusalem's security which is most significant. Since we have already seen that the assertion regarding the work of the angel of Yahweh in destroying the Assyrians in the year 701 (2 Kings 19:35) is quite out of line with its context in the account B2, we have good reason for concluding that it has only been introduced into the narrative of the events of that year at a comparatively late stage. It marks a high point in the growth of the tradition concerning the way in which Jerusalem was spared from destruction by Sennacherib, but, consequentially, changes substantially the perspective regarding the time when Yahweh's destruction of Assyria was thought to have taken place. It pointed back to Hezekiah's reign, instead of forward to that of Josiah, which was quite clearly the age in which Isaiah's threat against Assyria was originally expected to find fulfilment. The belief that Jerusalem would be providentially protected from Sennacherib in 701, which forms the basic focal point of both the B1 and B2 accounts in their original separate form, has become heightened to include an assertion that the Assyrian forces were not simply frustrated, but actually defeated, then. Evidently the editor who combined the B1 and B2 accounts, or possibly an even later scribe, felt that the story of what had taken place lacked a sufficiently dramatic portrayal of how the hand of God had been at work to protect Jerusalem. In consequence he introduced the note about the work of the angel of Yahweh. In the light of this uncovering of the way in which the narrative account has been subjected to a theological maximising of the emphasis upon Yahweh's intervention, we must accept the comment of 2 Kings 19:35 for what it is - a piece of theological colouring! It is quite mistaken therefore to attempt to rationalise it in order to find some mysterious happening to which it supposedly refers. Once this verse is set aside in this fashion we have no serious difficulty in recognising that the essential basis of the B1 and B2 accounts refers to the event of Hezekiah's surrender to Sennacherib in 701, of which we already have ample testimony. That the story has passed through a process of theological embellishment in the course of its composition is further shown by the way in which it has grown by the skilful combination of two essentially duplicate narrative accounts, and by the way in which the prophecy of 2 Kings 19:21-34 has been formulated from three separate elements. Overall we have every reason for concluding that the composition of the narrative must be ascribed to a circle of writers who stood very close to those who edited the prophecies of Isaiah during Josiah's reign. In a very real sense the narrative of 2 Kings 18:17-19:37 must be looked upon as a unique elaboration of Isaiah's prophecy of Isa. 10:5-15*.

Once we accept these conclusions regarding the date and provenance of the narrative of 2 Kings 18:17-19:37 (account B), we cease to have any serious difficulty in reaching a clear understanding of what happened in the year 701. Any need to posit a second confrontation between Hezekiah and Sennacherib, either in that year or later, is effectively removed altogether. If we piece together a combined picture of events we find that the following reconstruction emerges:

1. Sennacherib destroyed almost all the Judean towns and cities, but did not launch any direct assault upon Jerusalem, or press a siege against the city. He isolated it by building an earthwork which surrounded it, but, after many of Hezekiah's troops had deserted him, the latter surrendered.

2. Sennacherib received a substantial indemnity from Hezekiah.

3. Sennacherib confirmed Hezekiah on the throne of Judah, and this must be understood as a consequence of Assyrian policy, rather than as a sign of unexpected leniency towards Judah's king, or a result of his acting under any duress.

4. Sennacherib returned home to Nineveh, where he was eventually murdered (681 B.C.), without inflicting on Jerusalem the kind of savage destruction which other cities of Judah and Israel had experienced at the hands of the kings of Assyria.

This is the picture that results from the evidence of Sennacherib's Annals, account A (2 Kings 18:13-16) and account B (2 Kings 18:17-19:37). Not all the points appear in all the records, since each has undoubtedly recalled the event from a particular perspective. The question whether Sennacherib was compelled through some military necessity to make a quick settlement cannot be determined with certainty. It does not, however, affect the overall picture, since there is no real need to interpret Sennacherib's terms imposed on Hezekiah as a consequence of any special leniency. The need to retain some degree of political stability without the cost of maintaining a substantial Assyrian force in Judah adequately explains the terms that were offered and accepted. From the Old Testament side it was Jerusalem's escape from the destruction that had been inflicted on so many other cities of Israel and Judah, and upon so many other nations, that drew attention to the singular nature of the city's having been spared. It was in the retrospect of the age of Josiah, when Assyria's influence in Judah was at last weakening, that a special theological significance came to be discerned in what had happened. God had defended his own reputation and honour in protecting Jerusalem, and he had displayed the unique importance which he attached to the dynasty of David, a point which had earlier been set out by the prophet Isaiah (cf. Isa. 9:2-7).

The special character of the royal theology to which this Old Testament narrative account bears witness is further shown by the addition of two other stories, both of which have been related to the events of the year 701 B.C. These are to be found in 2 Kings 20, and the first of them concerns Hezekiah's sickness (2 Kings 20:1-11), the second to the sending of envoys from the Babylonian king, Merodach-bala-dan (Marduk-apal-idinna; 2 Kings 20:12-19). On examination it quickly becomes apparent that these two narratives have been included at this point precisely because they illustrate further the general theme of God's providential concern for the Davidic dynasty amd for Jerusalem /14/. What is most striking is that they have evidently been introduced into their present position in order to modify, and to tone down, the rather overdrawn note of assurance and confidence in Yahweh's protection that could be inferred from the account of Jerusalem's deliverence. Once the interpretation of what had happened in 701 had become generalised into an affirmation of the unique protection which Jerusalem and its Davidic king could expect to enjoy, then the dangers of complacency, and even of misunderstanding, had to be noted and corrected. In any case the fact of Josiah's unexpected death in the year 609, at the hands of Pharaoh Necho, must have aroused a very deep sense of shock that a Davidic king who had displayed such an exemplary zeal for God should have perished in such a fashion. Bearing this fact in mind, it is very easy to understand why the first of the stories which form a sequel to the narrative of Jerusalem's deliverance should have been added. This concerns an illness which Hezekiah suffered, which brought him close to death, but from which he was delivered through the action of God (2 Kings 20:1-11). In this Isaiah is first reported as having sent a message from God to the king, warning him that he was about to die (2 Kings 20:1). Upon receiving this news Hezekiah is said to have prayed a brief prayer which is very striking for its note of humble submission to God and its re-affirmation of the faithfulness which had marked all of Hezekiah's life (vv.2-3). There is no hint whatsoever of any note of repentance, since none is felt to be called for. Thereafter the prophet is reported to have sent a further word from God to the king, assuring him that his prayer had been heard and that fifteen years would be added to his life. A simple form of treatment is then indicated by Isaiah for the infection, which is now more closely identified as a boil. The fact that this treatment would lead to the king's recovery is then signified in a surprising way. There is to be a miraculous backward movement of a shadow of the setting sun on steps in the palace court (possibly a sun-clock).

The historical fact of the illness, and the problem posed by the miraculous nature of the sign that it would be healed, need not detain us. They are in themselves scarcely amenable to simple explanations. The point that matters from the perspective of our concern with the theology of the three Isaiah narratives is that the whole incident is related, by its date, directly to the account of the deliverance of Jerusalem from Sennacherib. According to 2 Kings 20:6 the healing of the king and the deliverance of Jerusalem were related events which God was to bring about for the same reason: his regard for the dynasty of David:

> And I will add fifteen years to your life. I will deliver you and this city out of the hand of the king of Assyria, and I will defend this city for my own sake and for my servant David's sake.
>
> (2 Kings 20:6).

The formula "for my own sake and for my servant David's sake" immediately recalls the closely similar expression in 2 Kings 19:34, where it appears in explanation of God's defence of Jerusalem from Sennacherib. Furthermore, the identification of Yahweh as "the God of David your father" (2 Kings 20:5) points to the same interest in the divine support for the Davidic dynasty. That these formulas indicate a central theme of the larger theology of history which governs the account of the monarchy has already been pointed out. Their repetition in this fashion, however, confirms our view that, rather than being faced here with additions from a Deuteronomistic editor, we have in these comments intrinsic features of the narratives. They point us to a circle of editors closely allied to the authors of the Deuteronomic writings.

Three: The Isaiah Narratives

The connection of Hezekiah's recovery from illness with the deliverance of Jerusalem is the most probable explanation of the figure of fifteen years added to the king's life. Since Hezekiah was known to have reigned for twenty-nine years (2 Kings 18:2), and the deliverance of Jerusalem was ascribed (erroneously) to the fourteenth year of his reign (2 Kings 18:3), a simple deduction has been made by the narrator. As with the story of Jerusalem's deliverance, so also this narrative clearly stands at some distance in time from the event it records. Yet it is abundantly evident that the author of the story wished to associate the report of the providential nature of the king's recovery from illness with the fact of Jerusalem's escape in 701. Evidently the one event was believed to be capable of shedding light upon the other. When we come to ask what this special illumination is, we are immediately struck by the remarkable fact that, in a moment of crisis, the king demonstrated his faithfulness and his total lack of any need for an expression of repentance. The theme of the narrative is evidently that of "the blessedness of the good king", a point which is brought out strongly by the king's simple prayer of loyalty and submission to God (2 Kings 20:3). Hezekiah had served God "with a whole heart" throughout his life. Is this not intended as a point of supplementary clarification to show the nature of the protection afforded to Jerusalem in 701? It hints strongly in the direction of regarding this protection as exceptional, by showing that it could only be granted to a faithful king. It introduces an element of conditioning, by showing how exemplary had been the life and obedience to God shown by Hezekiah. The implication of this must surely be that, if no such obedience were forthcoming, Jerusalem could not be so sure of its divine support. The narrative brings out the need for loyalty and obedience on the part of the king, although it was no doubt based upon some incident recorded in the royal annals of Judah. It shows that, if Judah were to continue to receive the kind of protection which the simple interpretation of the narrative of Jerusalem's deliverance in 701 attested. then this could be relied upon only if certain conditions were fulfilled. With this we must certainly have a key to understanding the time at which the narrative has arisen. Almost certainly it has been composed after Josiah's death in 609, either during the reign of Jehoiakim (609-598) or of Zedekiah

(598-587). It shows how the theology that had been expressed in the original deliverance narrative came to be regarded as too simple, bordering on the complacent. That God would always act to protect Jerusalem "for his own sake and for the sake of his servant David" did not express the whole truth about the nature of the relationship which bound together God, king and city /15/.

If this suggestion regarding the second of the trilogy of Isaiah narratives is put forward with some caution, then no such doubt can be entertained about the third of them. This is the account of the visit to Jerusalem of emissaries from Merodach-baladan (2 Kings 20:12-19). Here it is indubitably clear that the incident has been mentioned, and handled in the way that it is, in order to take account of the fact that an event had already happened which seemed to contradict the assurances of God's protection for Jerusalem. This event is referred to with such a degree of precision and detail in vv.17-18 that there is no difficulty in identifying what it is:

> Behold, the days are coming, when all that is in your house, and that which your fathers have stored up till this day, shall be carried to Babylon; nothing shall be left, says Yahweh. And some of your own sons, who are born to you, shall be taken away; and they shall be eunuchs in the palace of the king of Babylon.
> (2 Kings 20:17-18)

The reference must be to the surrender to the king of Babylon by Jehoiachin in 598, which was followed by the stripping of the temple and its treasures and the deportation to Babylon of the king and almost his entire household (2 Kings 24:12-16). In 598 Jerusalem and its royal house had suffered a defeat and humiliation which seemed to stand in contradiction to all the assurances and hopes which had surrounded them since the days of Josiah, and which were certainly older still in their ultimate origin. What had happened then cried out for explanation since it appeared to make nonsense of all the hopes which the accounts of Jerusalem's deliverance in Sennacherib's time had been intended to foster. It is this necessity to provide some explanation for an event which took place after 701 which accounts for the curious placing of the story where it is, out of proper chronological order. Although a precise date cannot be given for the coming to Jerusalem of emissaries from Merodach-baladan, the most probable is in connection with Hezekiah's revolt in the period 705-701. Their arrival was concerned with the negotiations for concerted action by several of Assyria's vassals in withdrawing support from the suzerain power. The only satisfactory alternative date would be to place the incident earlier still, between 713 and 711 /16/. Yet it has been placed where it is, after the narrative of Jerusalem's deliverance, because its theological purpose is to show that Yahweh had already determined not to give such unqualified protection to Jerusalem from the Babylonian threat as he had against the Assyrians. This also accounts for the extraordinary "lameness" of the reason given why such protection would not be forthcoming a second time. Hezekiah had shown the Babylonian emissaries all his treasures, although why this was wrong, and why Yahweh would punish him for having perpetrated this act of courtesy, is not made clear at all. The authors of the story themselves were undoubtedly looking for an explanation for an event which for them had already taken place, and which seemed to stand in such stark and frightening contrast to the deliverance which Hezekiah had earlier enjoyed. So far as they could see, this act of courtesy to the Babylonian emissaries was all that could explain such a catastrophe.

A third point about this story of the Babylonian emissaries is also of considerable interest for the understanding of the Isaiah narratives as a whole. This is the quite striking fact that its description of the punishment and humiliation that was to be inflicted on the Davidic dynasty as a result of Hezekiah's action quite explicitly points forward to what happened in 598, but says nothing of the more serious sufferings inflicted by the Babylonians in 587 /17/. Then Zedekiah was blinded, his sons killed, and he himself was taken prisoner to Babylon (2 Kings 25:6-7). The fate of Jerusalem and its temple was even worse, with the sanctuary itself being burned (2 Kings 25:9, 13-17). No further Davidic king was placed on the throne, so that this year effectively marked the end of the four hundred year rule of the dynasty of David over Israel and Judah. It is inconceivable that a circle of authors who were deeply concerned for the Davidic monarchy, and who believed that Yahweh had, in the past, acted "for the sake of his servant David", would have mentioned what happened in the year 598, but would fail to mention what took place later in 587, if this had in fact occurred by the time at which they wrote. There would appear to be only one explanation which can adequately account for the form that this third Isaiah narrative takes. It must have been written sometime after 598, but before 587. The suggestion that the event of 587 was all of a piece with that of 598, so that the authors may be regarded as simply having allowed the circumstances of the one event to indicate the consequences of both does not do justice to the markedly greater severity of the second defeat. The effect of this later surrender, with its concomitant destruction of Jerusalem, was so far-reaching as to change the perspective entirely. We can only draw the conclusion that this account of the visit of the Babylonian emissaries was composed after 598 but before 587, and that it was specifically intended from the outset to take account of the tragic events of that year with their special implications for the Davidic dynasty. It was therefore clearly intended, along with the story of Hezekiah's illness and recovery, to clarify and modify the assurances of Yahweh's special protection of Jerusalem and its Davidic monarchy which the earlier narrative of Jerusalem's deliverance in 701 had been designed to express. To this extent neither of the two later narratives in which Isaiah is involved are fully independent stories, but were composed with an intentional relationship to the earlier basic one which they serve to modify. In this light we can see how greatly the perspective changed after 587, and how significant it is that the happenings of that year are not taken into account in the overall presentation.

The original narrative of Jerusalem's deliverance in 701, which we have concluded was composed during Josiah's reign, gave a very reassuring and optimistic picture of the divine regard for Jerusalem and its Davidic monarchy which the events of that year were believed to demonstrate. Subsequently, and almost certainly after Josiah's death, a further incident was noted in order to show that Hezekiah was an exceptionally pious and faithful king. Beside this a further incident was narrated in order to bring out the recognition that the Davidic monarchy would not come through so unscathed in confrontation with the Babylonians as it had against the Assyrians. This is presented as already pre-

Three: The Isaiah Narratives

determined from as far back as Hezekiah's reign. Yet, in spite of these cautionary additions, the note of salvation and hope that is implicit in the original narrative is not abandoned. It is merely modified and subjected to certain conditions. The overall perspective that the combined trilogy of stories presents is that Jerusalem and the Davidic monarchy still have a formative role to play in God's purposes for his people Israel, even though this role must not be interpreted in a dogmatic, or unconditioned, way.

If this picture of the growth of the series of three narratives involving the prophet Isaiah is accepted, then we gain from them a valuable insight into the theology and political expectations which emerged during Josiah's reign, but which thereafter required substantial modification as a result of the misfortunes which befell Judah during the next three reigns. The overall perspective of the connected trilogy therefore is that of Zedekiah's reign, and there are indications which suggest that the authors considered that by this time the religious and political situation in Judah had stabilised itself /18/. As we know now, in the hindsight of what took place in 587, this was not the case, and both Jerusalem and its Davidic king were to face even worse misfortunes under Zedekiah than Jehoiachin had done. Nevertheless what we learn overall from these three stories, which are highly unusual on account of their concern with a major prophetic figure, provides an important glimpse into the political theology of certain circles in Jerusalem who undoubtedly stood close to the court.

When we come to enquire after the precise identity and aims of the authors of these narratives we can do little more than note two main facets of their literary associations. On the one hand they were evidently greatly interested in the prophecies of Isaiah, as is shown by the close similarities and connections which can be seen to exist between the form, theme and ideas of these narratives and those of the Josianic redaction of that prophet's book. Yet to call them "Isaiah's disciples" would be to speculate about the nature of their relationship to the prophet, and to ignore too many of the differences which characterise their outlook and distinguish it from that which we know of the prophet himself /19/. Overall the ideology of the narratives is too pro-monarchic, too confident of Yahweh's assurances to Judah, and too willing to ignore the sharp criticisms which Isaiah passed on the ruling circles in Jerusalem (cf. Isa. 5:8-23; 10:1-4), for this to be likely. In any case the very claim that there ever existed a continuing band of Isaianic disciples is an unwarranted speculation, which rests largely on a misinterpretation of Isa. 8:16.

The other literary connection of the authors of the Isaiah narratives is with the Deuteronomistic History in which the three stories are now preserved. We shall have occasion later to consider the question of the time and circumstances in which the trilogy of narratives was incorporated into the larger work. Yet there are several indications which suggest that those who penned these reports of events in Hezekiah's reign themselves stood very close to the authors of the great historical work which covers the books from Joshua to 2 Kings. The most obvious and noteworthy of these connections concerns the great importance which that work as a whole attaches to the special relationship between Yahweh and the house of David (2 Sam. 7:1-17; 1 Kings 8:16,24f.; 9:5; 11:12; 2 Kings 8:19; 21:7) /20/. This concern with the house of David provides a kind of <u>leitmotiv</u> which runs through the whole history. Significantly too it accounts for several features involving the distinctive structure and arrangement of the material. So also do the themes of Jerusalem and its temple play a large role in the history, while the work of prophets is regarded very highly even though, with the exception of Isaiah, none of the great prophetic figures of the period, of whom we have books, is mentioned by name. There are good reasons therefore why we should link the authors of the three Isaiah narratives very closely with the authors of the Deuteronomistic History into which they have been set. In fact the prominent position now given to the story of Jerusalem's deliverance in 701, contrasting so sharply with the fall of the Northern Kingdom and the surrender of Samaria, shows that a great importance was attached to the contents of these three stories by the authors of the larger work.

That some genuine link existed between the authors of the three Isaiah narratives and the original prophet may be upheld, as we can see from the way in which the prophet's book has been redacted. Much closer, however, are the links with the age of Josiah and with the Deuteronomic movement

Three: The Isaiah Narratives

which emerged at that time. Some of the wider implications of this may be considered later. Before undertaking this investigation it is necessary that we should consider an important exegetical problem which we noted earlier, but which we have so far left largely on one side. This concerns the origin and development of the so-called "Zion tradition", which, since the work of G. von Rad, has been regarded as a major influence upon the prophet Isaiah and the record of what took place in 701.

Chapter 4

ISAIAH AND THE ZION TRADITION

We have already pointed out at the beginning of our study
that one of the most influential features of recent
interpretation of the preaching of Isaiah has been the extent
to which he has been regarded as influenced by the Jerusalem
cult tradition. We may cite the words of G. von Rad who has
been in the forefront of those scholars who have advocated
an interpretation on this assumption: "It can be shown, of
course, that, wide-ranging and comprehensive as his message
is, it rests on a quite small number of religious concepts, all
of them furnished him by tradition, and in particular by the
Jerusalem tradition" /1/. The analysis of this Jerusalem
tradition, however, and the possibility of its connection with
the preaching of Isaiah, and even more directly with the
record of what took place in 701, goes back to the work of
scholars earlier than G. von Rad. In 1921 S. Mowinckel could
write in regard to the narrative of Jerusalem's deliverance
from Sennacherib: "The largely unhistorical account of a
catastrophe which took place in a single night, and which
destroyed Sennacherib's army before Jerusalem, 2 Kings
18:17-19:37, is nothing other than a carrying over of our
cult-legend onto historical persons and events" /2/. Hence,
even without positing so strong an influence of the Jerusalem
tradition upon the prophet himself, such as von Rad has
advocated, Mowinckel could regard the narrative record of
the city's escape as having arisen by way of an adaptation of
an ancient cult-legend. It was entirely in line with this that
he could also conclude that the preservation of Isaiah's
message among the circle of his "disciples" took place in the
closest and most direct connection with the cultic personnel
of Jerusalem /3/.

It is against the background of such claims as these that
the conclusions that we have reached in regard to Isaiah's
preaching at the time of Hezekiah's revolt against Sennacherib and the origin of the narrative of 2 Kings 18:17-19:37

must be considered. Is it possible that the secondary "prophecies" concerning the destruction of Assyria have been developed from Isaianic sayings under the impact of this Jerusalem cult-legend? Has the formation of the narrative account of Jerusalem's deliverance been assisted by the existence in the city of such a distinctive cultic tradition? Before we can attempt to resolve these questions we must consider the evidence for the existence of such a distinctive "Zion tradition", as it has come to be called, and what it has been thought to comprise.

The origins of this fresh approach to the interpretation and significance of the Jerusalem cultic themes and ideology must be traced back to the work of Hermann Gunkel on the Psalter, and in particular to his isolation of a special category of hymnic psalms which he called Zionslieder - Songs of Zion /4/. These especially concern Pss. 46, 48 and 76, although precisely which psalms may be held to belong within this category is a relatively secondary consideration. Certainly it is these three which are the primary ones for the uncovering of the special "Zion tradition". In his commentary on the Psalms, A.F. Kirkpatrick in 1902 /5/ could, as we have already noted, regard it as a "virtual certainty" that Pss. 46. 47 and 48 had originated in the wake of the marvellous deliverance that Jerusalem had experienced in the face of Sennacherib's threat in 701. Yet, in the decisively new approach to the interpretation of the Psalms advocated initially in his Ausgewählte Psalmen, Hermann Gunkel could regard Ps. 46 as an eschatological song, the theme of which was the eschatological world-drama which is also reflected in the preaching of the prophets /6/. In consequence the description of the defeat of hostile nations and the destruction of weapons of war which the psalm contains was an eschatological hope, which was ultimately of mythological origin:

> Come, behold the works of Yahweh,
>   how he has wrought desolations in the earth.
> He makes wars cease to the end of the earth;
>   he breaks the bow, and shatters the spear,
>   he burns the chariots with fire!
> "Be still, and know that I am God.
>   I am exalted among the nations,
>   I am exalted in the earth!"

Yahweh of hosts is with us;
the God of Jacob is our refuge.
(Ps. 46:8-11)

When the distinctive modifications of S. Mowinckel's cult-mythological interpretation of Pss. 46, 48 and 76 were added to this, the possibility emerged of an entirely different view of the order of the relationship between the Zion psalms and the tradition of the deliverance of Jerusalem in 701. This is the view which Mowinckel himself advocated: that it was the currency of this cult-mythological theme in Jerusalem which has led to the highly elaborated, and largely unhistorical, account of what happened to the city when it was confronted by Sennacherib's armies. It is, however, no great step from this position to that which regards the prophet himself as having been deeply affected by the distinctive Zion tradition of Jerusalem. Basically the same position that von Rad defends regarding Isaiah's indebtedness to this Zion tradition is argued for by E. Rohland /7/, while H.-J. Kraus /8/, A.R. Johnson /9/ and F. Stolz /10/ have developed along different paths the contention that the essentials of the tradition are to be traced back to the pre-Israelite inhabitants of the city. Rohland outlines the following four main elements in the tradition /11/:

1. Mount Zion is to be identified with Mount Zaphon, the "highest mountain" of Canaanite mythology.
2. The river of paradise flows out from these, so that the spring Gihon was associated with this (cf. Gen. 2:13; 1 Kings 1:45).
3. The conflict between the Creator God and the unruly waters of chaos took place there, with God defeating the waters.
4. This conflict with the powers of chaos was given a historical form in an assertion of Yahweh's victory over rebellious nations and their rulers at the gates of Jerusalem.

To these four main elements H. Wildberger has suggested that a fifth should be added, namely that of the pilgrimage of the nations to Mount Zion (as portrayed in Isa. 2:2-4 = Mic. 4:1-5) /12/. Unnamed nations come to offer their tribute to Yahweh and to accept the justice of his rule. Certainly there is sufficient evidence to indicate that this pilgrimage theme

Four: The Zion Tradition

came to be closely linked with the rest of the purported Zion tradition. The question that remains at issue, in this as with many of the features which have been ascribed to this "Zion tradition", concerns the chronology of its development. So far as the assumed Canaanite-Jebusite origin of the tradition is concerned, the circularity of the arguments that are used to support this, and the very hypothetical nature of the reconstructions of the original form of the tradition, require us to regard such conclusions with extreme caution /13/. In regard to the preaching of Isaiah and the related question of the origin of the narrative of Jerusalem's deliverance in 701, it is element (4) that particularly concerns us. However we explain its origin, the belief that Jerusalem would be the place where Yahweh overthrew rebellious nations and their rulers is held to have affected the interpretation of the events of 701. The issue is not that of when we are to date Pss. 46, 48 and 76 in relation to the prophet Isaiah, but rather the contention that the belief that rebellious rulers would be defeated outside Jerusalem has been adapted by the prophet or his interpreters to the unique historical situation of 701. It could certainly be that the psalms themselves are of later date than the tradition which is reflected within them.

From our own analysis of the preaching of Isaiah in relation to the events of 701 we have ruled out the possibility that this prophet did in fact assert any such firm expectation that Jerusalem would be delivered from Sennacherib, or that the city could be regarded as inviolable through its divine protection. Yet this does not entirely resolve all the issues which are raised by the hypothetical reconstruction of the Zion tradition, since we have seen that there are clearly passages of a secondary nature present in the book of Isaiah which present such an expectation. It would assist us in no little measure in looking for the origin of the underlying conviction which pervades these sayings if there had existed in Jerusalem such a popularly held Zion tradition. We should then have good reason for concluding that the authors of these sayings in the book of Isaiah, and of the narrative of 2 Kings 18:17-19:37, had drawn upon this tradition in formulating their own perspective on the confrontation between Hezekiah and Sennacherib. Yet even at this level the conclusions that we are entitled to draw from the available evidence are more complex than has usually been recognised, and the varying elements of the evidence are less homogeneous than has frequently been assumed to be the case. Quite evidently the unique character of the story of Jerusalem's deliverance, and the virtual impossibility that exists of explaining its origin on the basis of known events, has encouraged the view that there must have been a special tradition current from which its main features could have been taken. Then it has not been difficult to put together a number of sayings and ideas from a variety of sources in the Old Testament, and beyond it, which can be assembled together to make up such a Zion tradition. This is then the object of a hypothetical reconstruction, not the substance of any one clearly preserved text in which the tradition, as it existed in its supposed original form, is plainly set out. The most advanced effort in this direction is undoubtedly that by F. Stolz /14/, which very much resembles a situation in which pieces from several jig-saw puzzles have been mixed together and the attempt has been made to fit them all into some coherent shape on the assumption that they all belong to the same puzzle. What we must first do is to draw the pieces together into their separate collections and to see where they fit within these, before attempting anything more ambitious by way of fitting them all into a grander scheme. We cannot avoid noticing that there is an inevitable circularity in an argument which constructs the hypothesis of the Zion tradition in order to explain the difficulties which are present in the Isaiah tradition.

Certainly our criticism of the claim that certain sayings which are now to be found in the book of Isaiah, together with the narrative of 2 Kings 18:17-19:37, are dependent on the Zion tradition must begin at a fundamental level. Is it even clear that the Zion tradition, as it has been reconstructed, certainly antedates the time of the prophet Isaiah? We cannot enter into a full debate on the claims for the Jebusite origin of such a mythological tradition, and its pre-Israelite entry into Israel. It is not to be denied that the three main Zion psalms, Pss. 46, 48, 76, do show a heavy degree of mythological imagery and language, with some explicit references to Canaanite titles. The threat from the "waters" (Ps. 46:2-3), the "river" which brings joy in Ps. 46:4 /15/, and the identification of Mount Zion with Mount Zaphon (Ps. 48:1-2) /16/, are mythological features, and the title

Four: The Zion Tradition

'Elyon = "Most High" (Ps. 46:4) points to the Canaanite sphere of religion /17/. Yet having granted these points, there is little clear support, other than through an ill-defined association of themes, to indicate that the defeat of the unnamed "kings" was a historicisation of the myth of the subjugation of the waters of chaos at the creation of the world. Nor is the reference to the destruction of the ships of Tarshish in Ps. 48:7 a clear adaptation of a myth, or of an element from one. We must certainly admit that the Zion psalms show traces of a strong influence from Canaanite religious language and ideas, but this is true of a great many psalms. It must now be regarded as certain that the establishing of the Israelite cultus in Jerusalem drew heavily upon an even older religious life and thought-world of the ancient Orient. Much of this may have entered directly from the Jebusites /18/, but this is hardly true of all of it. There are several traces of a broadly Mesopotamian-Canaanite religious influence, but there are clearly present also signs of a dependence on ideas and language from the culture and religion of ancient Egypt. The pursuit of origins in this fashion can only be an uncertain and hypothetical under-taking, yet one point is of great importance. There is no reason at all to suppose that the Israelite cult of David's time was little more than a Yahwistic adaptation of the old Jebusite cult. Rather there are good reasons for believing that something genuinely new was created, certainly by the time of the building of Solomon's temple, which was free to draw openly from a very broadly spread tradition of archi-tecture and cultus.

The claim that the religious developments of David's and Solomon's reigns, with all their evident marks of "syncretism", were simply adapted from the old Jebusite cultus /19/, ignores the potential for novelty that lay within the new situation. We need not press further the uncertain-ties and weaknesses that are inherent in the supposed Jebusite origin of the Zion tradition, which is held to have been current in the Jerusalem of Isaiah's day. What we find are clear signs that the Israelite cultus of Jerusalem held special beliefs about the presence of Yahweh in the sanctuary there. The celebration of his power was upheld by reference to widely attested divine titles and cultic themes which bear a strongly mythological character. The inhabitants of Jeru-

salem were certainly encouraged to believe that their God
would protect them in time of war and bless them with peace
and prosperity. Yet these ideas were fundamental elements in
almost all the major cult-traditions of the ancient Orient.
There is little to indicate that Jerusalem was especially
unique in this regard. If we had fuller information about the
ancient cults of Bethel, Shechem and elsewhere we should no
doubt find that there were many features in which they were
closely similar to that of Jerusalem. There is no reason why
we should be especially surprised therefore that the old
Jerusalem cultus was linked with a mythology about a sacred
mountain and that it identified the forces of rebellion and
chaos with primeval waters. Nor is it at all surprising that
the citizens of Jerusalem believed that their God would guard
and protect them in time of war, since this must have been
one of the most deeply embedded of all early man's religious
convictions. What we lack, and yet what is so essential to the
proper understanding of the way in which the Zion tradition
has been held to have influenced the Isaiah tradition at some
level or other, is a clear indication that Jerusalem was held
to be different, and more privileged, than any other city of
Israel. It is not just the currency of mythological ideas about
God's presence in Jerusalem and his protection of the city
that we need to trace, but the clear assertion that these were
uniquely assured for Jerusalem above all the other cities of
Israel.

It is at this point that we can bring into the discussion a
point that has been briefly noted by H.M. Lutz /20/, and more
fully evaluated and explored by J.J.M. Roberts /21/. This is
that the theme of the defeat by Yahweh of rebellious kings
and their peoples from Jerusalem is very clearly present in
the Davidic royal psalm, Psalm 2. Once we bear in mind that
the authors of the Isaiah narratives of 2 Kings 18:17-20:19,
both explicitly (2 Kings 19:34; 20:6) and by implication,
attributed Jerusalem's deliverance in 701 to the relationship
of Yahweh to the Davidic dynasty, we discover the great
importance of this royal motif to the development of the
Zion tradition. We may conclude with reasonable confidence
that Ps. 2 is a Judahite coronation psalm of the pre-exilic
period /22/. It pictures quite graphically the plotting of
rebellious rulers and their attempt to cast off the yoke of

submission to the Davidic ruler:

> The kings of the earth set themselves,
>   and the rulers take counsel together,
>   against Yahweh and his anointed, saying,
> "Let us burst their bonds asunder,
>   and cast their cords from us."
> (Ps. 2:2-3)

Such rebellion is then shown to be doomed to failure because of the intervention of Yahweh who will frustrate and defeat such rebellious intentions:

> "You shall break them with a rod of iron,
>   and dash them in pieces like a potter's vessel."
> Now therefore, O kings, be wise;
>   be warned, O rulers of the earth.
> Serve Yahweh with fear,
>   with trembling kiss his feet,
> lest he be angry, and you perish in the way;
>   for his wrath is quickly kindled.
> Blessed are all who take refuge in him.
> (Ps. 2:9-11)

The promise is addressed to the Davidic ruler, who is the "you" addressed in v.9. The general similarity of the description of the rebellious rulers given here to that contained in the so-called Zion psalms (especially Ps. 46:6 and 48:4) suggests that the same broad context of ideas and allusion is present in all of them. Hence the description of the overthrow of the rebellious forces that is pictured in Pss. 46:8-10; 48:5-6 and 76:3-6 is most probably to be explained as a reference to the removal of a potential, rather than an actual, threat. Almost certainly then we are presented here with essentially variant expressions of one basic tradition, which related to the imperialistic claims that had at one time arisen in connection with the emergence of the Davidic-Solomonic empire /23/. The relatively brief period during which this had flourished as a historical reality in no way led to the discarding, or suppression, of such a tradition once the extent of the political hegemony of Israel and Judah became greatly reduced. This would serve to explain why the enemies appear as rebels, rather than as a major threatening world-power. There are strong reasons therefore for concluding that the theme of the Conflict with the Nations, with its portrayal of the defeat of rebellious nations by Yahweh to bring in an age of peace, was an aspect of the royal Davidic ideology which had become established in Jerusalem. How early it emerged and whence it drew its major motifs and ideas can only be a matter of reasoned conjecture. Yet there can scarcely be any cause for hesitating to conclude that it belonged to the Jerusalem cultus from a very early state, very possibly reaching as far back as David's own time, but more probably entering with the great elaboration of cultus that took place with the building of the temple /24/. Whence it drew its inspiration cannot be certainly determined, since the whole question of the ideology of kingship which flourished with the Davidic dynasty in Jerusalem is still the subject of much discussion. The general association of the tradition with some features of a mythological character which are well attested in the Mesopotamian sphere would indicate that we cannot rule out a Canaanite-Jebusite source of such a theme in Israel /25/. On the other hand there is important evidence in the Judean royal titles, especially that concerning the king's divine "sonship" /26/, the Judean coronation ritual /27/, and also the administrative structure of the Davidic kingdom /28/, to show us that a significant measure of Egyptian influ- ence was felt in Israel at this time. Nor can we overlook a certain similarity of function and content between the threat to rebellious rulers contained in the Conflict with the Nations motif and certain features of the vassal-treaties which have been heavily discussed in connection with other aspects of Israel's religious development /29/.

We may therefore conclude that it is virtually certain that this motif entered into Israel as a part of the Davidic royal ideology which flourished in the cultus of Jerusalem. There is no reason therefore why we should continue to look for its origin in a hypothetically reconstructed Jebusite mythology concerning a sacred mountain. Certainly when we come to consider the overall make-up of the Jerusalem cult-tradition of pre-exilic Judah we find that it appears to have contained a variety of images and themes, broadly mythological in their character, which were combined together into some sort of whole. To conclude that the Conflict with the Nations motif was a historicised form of the myth of the defeat of the waters of chaos /30/ is to go beyond the evidence that we have, and to insist that one feature was intentionally used to replace, or modify, another. That this was the case is entirely unsupported by the evidence. What we do find is that the Conflict with the Nations theme fits quite appropriately in a cultic tradition which was, from its Israelite inception, associated with a claim to hegemony over a number of surround ing subject kingdoms. The fact that this political situation existed for Israel only very briefly in no way lessens the strength of the claim that it was precisely this situation which gave rise to several fundamental features of the Davidic royal ideology. To call such an affirmation regarding Yahweh's threat to thwart the intentions of the rebellious kings an eschatological expectation, as H. Gunkel did /31/, is greatly to exaggerate the conscious time-scale in which it was applied. It was not pointing to one far-off event, but to any potential situation in which its warnings might be necessary. We may broadly accept that it may be appropriately described as mythological, although even this description tells us less about the origin, form and function of its language than we might suppose. Certainly there is no reason for thinking that mythology and history were contrasting, or interchangeable, categories of thought. The shattering of the "ships of Tarshish" in Ps. 48:7 may well be a recollection of an actual historical event.

If we accept that the theme of the defeat of hostile and rebellious nations was a part of the Davidic royal ideology of Jerusalem, then two features of our examination of its application to the tradition of what happened in 701 gain in illumination. In the first place we have already noted that the authors of the Isaiah narratives ascribe the reason for the city's miraculous protection from Sennacherib to Yahweh's regard for David, which suggests that such an idea was already current when these narratives were composed. This belief in the special divine protection that was to be afforded to Jerusalem "for the sake of David" would then very plausibly find its explanation as a contemporary adaptation of the Conflict with Rebellious Nations motif, which formed a part of the Davidic royal ideology.

The second feature that is illuminated by this recognition of the Davidic connection of the Conflict motif concerns the distinctive origin of those sayings in the book of Isaiah which G. von Rad and others have ascribed to the influence of the

Isaiah and the Deliverance of Jerusalem

"Zion tradition" upon the prophet. This particularly concerns such passages as Isa. 8:9-10; 14:24-27; 17:12-14 and 29:5-6, where the destruction of hostile forces that threaten Jerusalem is described. From our own examination of these passages it will be clear that we have shown that they do not derive from the prophet Isaiah himself, but from a redactional circle who edited and expanded the prophet's sayings during the reign of Josiah. Hermann Barth has termed this the "Assyrian Redaction" /32/. That the content of these sayings shows a considerable degree of similarity with the imagery and general intent of the Conflict motif is not to be denied. It could well be, therefore, that it is this redactional circle which has been very strongly affected by the tradition of this motif. In part this would appear to have been the case, although we must note one significant point. This is to be seen in the foundational character of the accession oracle of Isa. 9:2-7 in the literary formation and development of these redactional sayings. Against Hermann Barth we have argued that this prophecy does derive from Isaiah, and was delivered on the occasion of the accession of Hezekiah to the throne of Judah. It is within this oracle, which reflects several traditional themes of the Davidic royal ideology, as A. Alt has shown /33/, that the Conflict motif appears quite prominently:

> For the yoke of his burden,
> and the staff for his shoulder,
> the rod of his oppressor,
> thou hast broken as on the day of Midian.
> For every boot of the tramping warrior in battle tumult
> and every garment rolled in blood
> will be burned as fuel for the fire.
>
> (Isa. 9:4-5)

It is particularly this aspect of the accession oracle that is taken up by the redactors in their application to the situation of Sennacherib's threat to Jerusalem (cf. Isa. 10:26-7; 14:25b). This further corroborates the contention that it was the presence of this Conflict motif in the Davidic royal ideology, and its adoption in the authentic preaching of the prophet Isaiah, which encouraged the general style and character of the "Assyrian Redaction" of his prophecies. In fact it would appear that it was a very formative and significant factor in the production of such a redaction. If this is so then we reach a very significant point where the lines of evidence converge. From a comparison of the presence of the main features of the Conflict with the Nations motif in both the Zion Psalms (Pss. 46, 48, 76) and the royal coronation psalm, Psalm 2, we concluded that the Conflict motif originated as a part of the Davidic royal ideology of the Jerusalem court and its related cultus. It was not a special feature of the sacred mountain mythology of Zion, although it came to be associated with it. Secondly, it appeared in the preaching of Isaiah in his own prophetic use of the themes and imagery of the Davidic royal ideology and was taken up from there into the Assyrian Redaction of his prophecies. The major change that was required was that the forewarning of the defeat of rebellious subject nations should have been adapted to apply to a major imperialistic power which threatened the sovereignty of Judah. From this we can see that in the development of this redactional material in the book of Isaiah the interpretation that was placed upon the unique situation which had existed in confrontation with Assyria came to be extended into a general doctrine regarding the divine protection that would be afforded to Jerusalem in the face of any oppressor. Thereby a widely applicable "doctrine of inviolability" came to be built up out of an interpretation that was imposed upon an individual historical situation. A very clear indication of the way in which this took place is provided by the way in which the passage Isa. 29:7-8 has been appended to 29:5-6. Both of these passages must be ascribed to the Assyrian Redaction of the book, but most probably in two separate stages, although we need not suppose that a long interval of time separated the two compositions. Isa. 29:7-8 quite consciously broadens and generalises the threat of destruction upon Jerusalem's oppressors. What had at first been directly intended to refer to the threat from Sennacherib's armies was extended into a threat against any nation that ventured to oppress Jerusalem:

And the multitude of all the nations that fight
    against Ariel
all that fight against her and her stronghold
    and distress her,
shall be like a dream, a vision of the night.

Isaiah and the Deliverance of Jerusalem

As when a hungry man dreams he is eating
and awakes with his hunger not satisfied,
or as when a thirsty man dreams he is drinking
and awakes faint, with his thirst not quenched,
so shall the multitude of all the nations be
that fight against Mount Zion.

(Isa.29:7-8)

The doctrine of the inviolability of Jerusalem, therefore, which several scholars have come to regard as a central feature of the so-called "Zion tradition", must rather be understood as a particular adaptation of the interpretation placed upon what happened in 701. It was not an original part of the Jerusalem cultic tradition, but rather a belief that came to be introduced into it at a particular time by a very distinctive circle. In part this circle drew upon the motif of the subjugation of rebellious nations from the royal ideology and the way this had been taken up in the preaching of Isaiah. Most of all, however, the doctrine of inviolability associated with the city stemmed from what was believed to have happened in 701 and the divine purpose that was believed to be revealed in this. Perhaps more precisely, in view of our examination of the origin of the sayings which reflect it in the book of Isaiah and the composition of the Isaiah narrative of 2 Kings 18:17-19:37, it derived from the larger experience of Jerusalem at the hands of the Assyrians in the last half of the eighth century B.C. Where the Northern Kingdom of Israel had been defeated and progressively reduced to ruin, and even Judah had been reduced to a fraction of its former size with almost all its towns and cities ravaged, Jerusalem had somehow been spared. This appeared to be by a special act of divine providence, which had come to be interpreted as miraculous, and which marked out the fate of Jerusalem from all the other cities and towns of greater Israel. It is this historical perspective, looking back over a third of a century of political disasters, which singled out Jerusalem from these other cities and sanctuaries.

The doctrine of Jerusalem's inviolability therefore, emerged, not as an adaptation of an ancient myth, but as an interpretation of a series of historical events, and focused most directly upon Hezekiah's confrontation with Sennacherib. To ascribe it to the "Zion tradition" is misleading on two counts. In the first place it suggests that the doctrine

Four: The Zion Tradition

already existed before Isaiah's time, which we have seen not to be the case. Secondly, such a title places the emphasis upon its association with the mythology of a sacred mountain, rather than with the royal Davidic ideology, which is how the Old Testament literature clearly understands it. Seen from this point of view we can recognise that the belief in Zion's inviolability was a generalisation of the divine purpose to which the fact of Jerusalem's escape from destruction by Sennacherib was ascribed. Its roots lay in the royal traditions of the city, and their special association with the dynasty of David, and in particular in the belief in the special relationship which was held to bind Yahweh and his protection closely to the Davidic family. Insofar as there is discernible an older, ancient Near Eastern, mythological origin to the belief, this must be sought in the elaborate royal ideologies which abounded in the ancient world. Yet in reality, as we have seen, this mythological imagery provided only a small part of what was, more directly, a historical and theological interpretation of Jerusalem's experience at the hands of the Assyrians during Hezekiah's reign.

When we put together these various pieces of evidence regarding the origin of the belief in Jerusalem's inviolability, and its relationship to other aspects of the Jerusalem cult-tradition, we arrive at a very different conclusion from that which has become widely current in recent expositions of Isaiah. Far from the preaching of this prophet presupposing a fully formed "Zion tradition", we find the opposite to be the case, and the most prominent feature of this so-called "Zion tradition" to be a consequence of that prophet's ministry. Yet even this conclusion must be set in perspective, since it is primarily the interpretation and development of Isaiah's preaching at the hands of the "Assyrian Redactors" of Josiah's age which saw the growth of the belief in Zion's unique umbrella of divine protection. It was essentially an interpretation, made in the perspective of Josiah's reign, of events which had taken place more than half a century earlier in the reign of Hezekiah.

It also becomes apparent that the belief in Zion's inviolability "for the sake of Yahweh's servant David" did not stand in isolation, but rather was a part of a more comprehensive ideology which found its focal point in the Davidic dynasty. It belonged to a very extensive religious interpretation of Israel's experience at the hands of the Assyrians.

Isaiah and the Deliverance of Jerusalem

Royal ideology, prophecy and the political ambitions of Judah were all drawn together in this wide-ranging belief in the special role that Jerusalem-Zion was to play in Yahweh's plan for his people Israel.

In the light of these conclusions we may draw attention to two features regarding the belief in Jerusalem's inviolability and its relationship to the purported Zion tradition which are of considerable significance for the interpretation of prophecy. This is especially important for the prophecies of Jeremiah and Ezekiel, and also for the development of a major stream of Old Testament theological understanding. The first of these concerns the fact that this belief in the special divine protection which was believed to have been guaranteed to Jerusalem flourished for only a relatively short period /34/. It can scarcely have developed much before the first half of Josiah's reign, and certainly it must have begun to appear to be of doubtful validity soon after that king's untimely death in 609 B.C. We can discover something of the awakening doubt about its validity from a careful study of the two appended Isaiah narratives in 2 Kings 20:1-19. It was not therefore an ancient, and long cherished, belief from which the citizens of Jerusalem only gradually and slowly broke free. There is, as we have seen, no reason at all for thinking that either the prophet Isaiah, or his contemporary Micah, shared such a view, or preached to people for whom it would have been an incomprehensible rejection of dogma to suggest that Jerusalem might fall to a foreign oppressor. This was rather the situation that faced Jeremiah and Ezekiel in the sixth century, by which time the belief in Jerusalem's inviolability had gained currency.

The second point concerns the connection between this belief and the great reform which took place in Josiah's reign in the years 623-622 B.C. It has become increasingly recognised as a result of the extensive modern examination of the origins of the Deuteronomic movement that the great reform of Josiah's reign was itself the religious outgrowth of a deep change in the political ideology of Judah during the early years of Josiah /35/. The throwing off of the burden of Assyrian domination, the removal of all political and religious evidence of this domination, and the recovery of new hope and revived political ambition in Judah as a result of the weakening of Assyrian power, were all indispensable prerequisites for Josiah's reform. As we can now see, even the

86

way in which the narrative record of 2 Kings 22:3-23:25 recounts this reform has tended to emphasise the religious aspects of it at the expense of its original political aims. Seen in the context of Josiah's reign, the specifically cultic aspects of the reform were relatively incidental to the underlying political intentions of its protagonists. Quite certainly, therefore, we can deduce that, when the extended written record of the reform was composed, the fragility, and possible failure, of the political dimension of the reform was frankly recognised. It is in part in compensation for this that the cultic and more distinctively spiritual side of it came to be stressed. These aspects were already beginning to be seen to be more permanent and enduring. If what we have discovered about the Assyrian Redaction of Isaiah's preaching and the related circle who composed the Isaiah narrative of 2 Kings 18:17-19:37 is upheld, then we have a valuable insight into the originating ideas and aims of the reformers of Josiah's time. The central allegiance to the Davidic dynasty, and the belief that it provided a viable explanation of why Jerusalem had been spared from Sennacherib formed the foundation of the beliefs of these reformers. What has come to be called somewhat misleadingly the "Zion tradition" was one expression of their faith, using the language and imagery of the ancient cult-hymns of Jerusalem.

It remains for us to consider the place of the Zion Psalms, Pss. 46, 48 and 76. Do these psalms themselves antedate the time of Isaiah, and if so do they not, in spite of our arguments, testify to the existence of the Zion tradition long before the time of Josiah? Or are we to suppose that they are also the product of the Josianic age, along with the Zion tradition which so many scholars have found expressed in them? The answers to these questions are not easy to reach since the available evidence for dating these psalms is so limited. However, if we work from the evidence of Ps. 48:2 with its reference to kingship, it would appear most plausible that these psalms do not in reality form a truly self-contained and separate group of hymns, as Gunkel suggested, but are royal psalms, closely allied to the other royal hymns of the pre-exilic Jerusalem cultus. This is how both S. Mowinckel and A.R. Johnson have understood them /36/, even though both scholars have also proceeded to conclude further from this that the whole "Zion tradition" belonged to the earliest form of the Jerusalem temple worship. Yet what we have in the content of these psalms is not a general doctrine of Jerusalem's inviolability, nor yet an affirmation of the final eschatological victory of Yahweh. Rather they express in a very distinctive fashion the hopes and aspirations for a kingdom of peace and righteousness which was associated with the Davidic dynasty. Such hymns, therefore, are most probably to be regarded as older than the time of Isaiah, but their content must be understood not as a special sacred mountain mythology associated with Mount Zion, but as a part of the royal ideology which was linked in Jerusalem with the Davidic dynasty. Overall therefore we can best regard the Zion psalms as giving voice to a particular aspect of the Jerusalem royal ideology.

If this view is effectively defensible, that the Zion ideology which has figured so prominently in recent study of the book of Isaiah was largely a product of Josiah's age, then we are given a remarkably favourable opportunity for seeing how such a faith could emerge. History, prophecy, as well as some aspects of an ancient royal ideology, have all contributed towards the growth of such a belief. Yet this faith, which took on such a confident form at a particular period of Israelite-Judean history, did not survive in its original form for very long. By 609 Josiah was dead in a seemingly futile bid to thwart the movement of Egyptian troops through his territory /37/. Within a further decade Jerusalem had been forced, after a prolonged siege, to surrender to the Babylonian armies and no angel had come from the skies to rescue the long-suffering people of that city. Within little over a decade more an even more devastating and catastrophic defeat overtook Jerusalem, and the last vestiges of the Zion tradition, as it has come to be called, were shown to be hollow and inadequate. In such fashion may the attempts to draw generalised dogmas from the contingencies of history be revealed as false and misleading. Yet in ways other than those of simple historical interpretation the growth and rise of the belief in Zion's inviolability had testified to something very significant about the nature of God and of his providence in human affairs /38/. This element of truth is very effectively captured by Martin Luther in his adaptation of the language of Ps. 46 in the hymn, "A safe stronghold our God is still". When lifted to a more transcendent and ultimate plane some of the motifs of the Zion ideology may be held to be eternally true, however much the uncomfortable contingencies of history appear to contradict them:

> God's word, for all their craft and force,
> One moment shall not linger,
> But, spite of hell, shall have its course;
> 'Tis written by his finger.
> And though they take our life,
> Goods, honour, children, wife,
> Yet is their profit small;
> These things shall vanish all.
> The city of God remaineth.

Chapter 5

THE DELIVERANCE OF JERUSALEM
IN THEOLOGICAL PERSPECTIVE

On the basis of the conclusions that we have reached so far, we are now able to put together a comprehensive thesis regarding the theological significance of what took place in 701 B.C. From both a prophetic and historiographical perspective it was clearly an event of great moment so far as the literature of the Old Testament is concerned. Even more prominent, however, is the particular cluster of theological beliefs to which it gave rise, and which have formed a central core of ideas within a wide area of Old Testament writings. On the basis of the literary and traditio-historical investigations we have undertaken there come to light a number of significant insights regarding the theological developments in Judah during the age of Josiah which are of great interest in tracing the origin and development of the Deuteronomic movement. Whereas it has become increasingly possible through recent study to trace the later development of this movement through the law book they have given to us, the Deuteronomistic History and the extant form of the book of Jeremiah, our own enquiries have led us to see some important aspects of its earlier growth /1/.

We may begin this broader review of the theological perspective relating to the deliverance of Jerusalem from Sennacherib by summarising our main conclusions. First of all, so far as the historical event iself is concerned, we may reiterate conclusions which were set out tentatively in our first chapter. What we have discovered since, in examining the preaching of Isaiah and the origin of the so-called "Zion tradition", has served to corroborate the position which we outlined there. Sennacherib's annals give a relatively full picture of the circumstances of Hezekiah's rebellion, the alliances on which it relied, and the punitive campaign by which Sennacherib quelled the revolt. Between the years 705 and 701 Judah faced a major political crisis in which

Five: Theological Perspective

dependence on Egyptian military aid was essential if the kingdom was to escape the wrath of the Assyrian king. In the outcome such aid was inadequate and Judah was severely punished, the details of that punishment being spelt out with vindictive gloating in the Assyrian record. After almost his entire kingdom had been reduced to ruins, Hezekiah surrendered when it was clear that further resistance was useless. By doing so he spared Jerusalem, the preparations for the siege of which had just begun, from experiencing the horrors and destruction which had been meted out to most of the rest of Judah and to Israel and other kingdoms in the course of earlier Assyrian campaigns.

That Jerusalem owed its deliverance to Hezekiah's timely surrender is borne out by the evidence of 2 Kings 18:13-16, which has come to be described by Old Testament scholars as Account A. That there was some more dramatic cause of Jerusalem's escape, however, has been widely accepted among Old Testament scholars by the presence of an Account B in 2 Kings 18:17-19:37. This ignores the fact of Hezekiah's surrender and, at a crucial point (2 Kings 19:35), ascribes the city's being delivered to the mysterious action of the angel of Yahweh. Detailed investigation of this Account B, however, shows that it is a composite narrative, written in its present form more than half a century after 701, with a strong tendency to heighten the emphasis on the sovereign control of events by Yahweh. Yet in its basis this Account B is also largely in agreement with the evidence from other sources about what took place in 701. Only in this single verse, which has arisen late in the process of literary development of the account, is there any mention at all of a destruction of the Assyrian army. It becomes evident then that Account B is a piece of theological narrative writing which has come to look back on the sparing of Jerusalem from Sennacherib as a singular manifestion of Yahweh's providential control of events and a special indication of his particular regard for Jerusalem and the Davidic dynasty. As narrative evidence it cannot be used to support the case, either that Sennacherib was tempted into making a second attempt on Jerusalem in 701, or that he was forced to undertake a further siege of the city in the course of some other campaign. The historical circumstances of the confrontation between Sennacherib and Hezekiah, therefore, and the course of events by which

Jerusalem escaped the horrors of prolonged siege and destruction, are all reasonably clear. One other point alone need be reiterated here. The fact that Hezekiah was allowed to retain his throne in Jerusalem after having rebelled against Assyria is sometimes regarded as a token of Sennacherib's leniency, for which some explanation, unmentioned in the Assyrian annals, may then be sought. Yet this is most probably a misinterpretation of the situation, and must rather be seen as a consequence of the broader Assyrian policy of using, whenever possible, vassal rulers from established native dynasties to adminster their provinces. The sheer administrative and logistical difficulties of controlling directly a host of far-flung subject states show why this was necessary. Almost certainly the widespread movement of populations in those provinces which were directly controlled as "internal" Assyrian dominions is a further reflection of these difficulties. We have no need therefore to look for a second campaign by Sennacherib, either in 701 or later, in order to explain the origin of the narrative of Account B. We may conclude with confidence therefore that there is no major historical problem that confronts us when considering the course of the Assyrian campaign which culminated in Hezekiah's surrender to Sennacherib in 701. What we have is primarily a literary and theological problem concerning the origin and purpose of the narrative of 2 Kings 18:17-19:37 which views in a very special light the fact that Jerusalem did not suffer the torments and destruction which befell most of the rest of Judah.

Of direct relevance to the attempt to trace the literary circles and theological ideas which have stimulated the composition of this distinctive narrative is an examination of the redaction of the preaching of the prophet Isaiah. There are now preserved in the book of this prophet a series of sayings which have a special bearing on the problem of the interpretation of what took place between Sennacherib and Hezekiah in 701. They foretell that the Assyrian forces which have threatened Judah will be frustrated. They even emphasise in an unusual fashion the fact that it will be the direct intervention of Yahweh which will bring this about. Hence they set aside the well-attested prophetic idiom by which the action of God is asserted when both the prophet and his hearers fully recognise that this will be achieved through human agents. Some more obviously direct divine action seems to be pointed to in these sayings. On examination, however, it becomes clear that these sayings are not from Isaiah himself, but have been composed after 701, in Josiah's reign. They have been composed by an unusual kind of "midrashic" exegetical elaboration of words and images drawn from Isaiah's authentic sayings in order to re-affirm his threat of punishment upon Assyria. In particular they are heavily dependent upon the two major prophecies of Isa. 9:2-6, concerning the salvation which Yahweh has affirmed for his people Israel through the Davidic dynasty, and Isa. 10:5-15*, concerning the coming punishment of the Assyrians for their blasphemous claim to have achieved their conquests through their own power. These sayings are part of a wider redactional elaboration of Isaianic sayings which make up what Barth has called the "Assyrian Redaction" of the book /3/. On the basis of sayings of Isaiah from the age of Hezekiah they provide a meaningful message for the period of Josiah's reign (640-609 B.C.).

This redaction has been built up around three major themes: Yahweh has not abandoned his people; there is nothing to fear from the Assyrians for their days of domination over Judah are quickly coming to an end; the salvation of Israel is assured through the Davidic dynasty. In this redaction of Isaiah's preaching the signal fact that Jerusalem had not fallen in 701, whereas no other major city of Judah or Israel had escaped the ravages of Assyrian attack, was looked upon as a mark of providential protection. When we came to reconsider the content and structure of the story of Jerusalem's deliverance in 2 Kings 18:17-19:37, we found that it showed a great many points of contact and similarity with this distinctive midrashic redaction of Isaiah's preaching. There are numerous verbal similarities, but most of all it is the fact that this narrative is built up around ideas and themes deriving from the prophecy of Isa. 10:5-15* that demonstrates such a connection. The major point of departure is that Isaiah himself had not at all related the threat of impending punishment on the Assyrian king to the situation of 701. In the narrative, however, it is this event, and the fact that Jerusalem was spared any battle or military defeat that has become the central focus of the story. The narrative itself can be seen to have been composed out of two separate accounts (B1 and B2), and there is evidence of a growth of theological direction. The original factual basis that there had been no battle for Jerusalem and that Sennacherib had returned home by the way that he came without destroying the city has, in the process of literary development, become the foundation of a theological doctrine. The final consequence of this is to be seen in the intrusion of the comment that the Assyrian army had experienced a severe defeat outside Jerusalem by the hand of the angel of Yahweh.

The belief that a special divine providence pertained to Jerusalem, so that the city was believed to be inviolable, has frequently been ascribed to the currency within the cultic traditions of the city, stemming from pre-Israelite days, of a distinctive "Zion tradition". That this tradition had a profound influence upon Isaiah, and in particular on the way in which the event of 701 came to be interpreted, has received a wide popularity in recent expositions of both the prophet and the account of Jerusalem's deliverance. Yet on examination it cannot be shown that those passages which have most commonly been held to display a dependence upon this "Zion tradition" really do so. Rather we have found that the tradition is more a consequence of the interpretation of what took place in 701 than its presupposition. Insofar as the language of the cult-hymns and ideology of Jerusalem have affected the way in which the story of Jerusalem's deliverance from the clutches of Sennacherib has been written up, it is the royal Davidic tradition that has contributed to this. Those features which have been claimed as the essential elements of the so-called "Zion tradition" are primarily the product of the way in which the event of 701 B.C. came to be remembered and interpreted. Beside the event itself two factors have lent colour and imagery to the tradition. One of these is the preaching of Isaiah, who had foretold the punishment of the Assyrians for their blasphemous arrogance, and the other is the royal Jerusalem tradition associated with the Davidic dynasty, which had its ultimate origins in the political mythology which surrounded many traditions of kingship in the ancient Orient. The belief that Jerusalem was subject to a unique guarantee of its defence and security, and had a unique role to play in the future government and blessedness of Israel, became a central part of the way in which the confrontation between

Five: Theological Perspective

Sennacherib and Hezekiah came to be remembered. As a wholehearted conviction it flourished briefly in Josiah's reign, before being subjected to a great deal of modification and theological development. The most obvious marks of this attempt to amend and clarify this distinctive royal Zion theology are to be found in the two further narratives which have been appended to the story of Jerusalem's deliverance in 2 Kings 20:1-19.

The conclusion that the narrative relating Jerusalem's marvellous deliverance from Sennacherib in 701 is a product of a distinctive royal Zion theology, which emerged during the reign of Josiah in the seventh century, is itself a valuable discovery. That there may have been a connection between the preaching of Isaiah and the origins of the Deuteronomic movement was long ago suggested by S. Mowinckel /4/, although the attempt to explain this connection through the work of "Isaiah's disciples" must be regarded as a speculative assumption rather than a demonstrable, or probable, conclusion. The fact of such a connection, however, is of greater importance than the manner in which we attempt to explain it. What appears justifiable from our own brief study is that there emerged a circle in Josiah's time, very close to the royal court, who maintained a very deep interest in the preaching of the prophet Isaiah and the fate of the Northern Kingdom of Israel. Their deepest conviction was that Judah had been divinely spared to be the heir of the once great kingdom of Israel, and that this act of divine mercy had been ordained on account of the special destiny which pertained to the Davidic dynasty /5/. This circle found a confirmation for these beliefs in the preaching of Isaiah, who had been active during the years in which the Northern Kingdom had fallen. More pointedly than this, however, this circle saw in Isaiah the great prophet of the oneness of Israel, and this conviction appears to be entirely justified by sayings which are preserved from that prophet. For their own day this company of Jerusalem monarchists saw in the weakening of Assyrian influence in Judah both the ending of a political nightmare and the fulfilment of Isaianic prophecy. They looked forward to the imminent dawning of a new day of political independence, prosperity and a restored Israel under a Davidic ruler (cf. Isa. 32:1-8). That they believed that Josiah himself would be the king under whom these hopes would be realised is in every way probable.

95

Isaiah and the Deliverance of Jerusalem

If these conclusions regarding the situation of the circle to whom we have ascribed the Josianic Redaction of the book of Isaiah and the composition of the narrative of Jerusalem's deliverance in 701 are correct, then this circle must have been very close to, if not identifiable with, the early leaders of the Deuteronomic movement /6/. The further implications of this we can consider shortly. For the moment it is sufficient to note that such a conclusion sheds a great deal of light upon one aspect of the great religious reform that took place under Josiah in 623 B.C. For long it has been a point of considerable debate how far this reform was a predominantly political movement, deeply anxious to remove from Judah every vestige of Assyrian domination and religious influence, and how far it was a more truly religious movement, bent on the internal purification of Israelite faith and worship /7/. Those circles to which we have drawn most attention, with their special interest in Isaiah's preaching, would point us firmly in the direction of recognising the strong political motivation of the reform. Undoubtedly there was a religious dimension to the changes that took place, but that they were originally undertaken as a part of a great resurgence of hope and a revival of political ambition in Judah seems certain. Josiah was set in the forefront of a movement which looked to recover the greatness of Israel, as it had existed in the days of David and Solomon when the kingdom had been united, and which the years of Assyrian domination had so severely checked. Now, with the ending of Assyria's power in sight, a new wave of hope and ambition re-asserted itself in Judah, finding great strength and support from the record of Isaiah's preaching. Such at least would appear to have been the aims and expectations which coloured the reformers of Josiah's time. The re-organisation of the cultus, and the removal of the remaining traces of idolatrous Canaanite practices, were largely a by-product of a movement which began with a larger, and more politically ambitious, goal. Those various attempts therefore to trace back the origins of the Deuteronomic movement to levitical circles whose primary aim was the purification and reorganisation of worship can scarcely be sustained /8/. Some group closer to the court and to the administrative affairs of the state are much more plausibly to be considered as the moving agents of the Deuteronomic reform. Yet it is clear that, as the

Five: Theological Perspective

movement developed, its political aims proved more and more to be abortive and it was compelled to attach greater importance to matters of a more directly religious and cultic significance. Certainly the account which we now possess of the course which the reform actually took (2 Kings 22-23), and which must largely date from after Josiah's death, fully reflects this more religiously oriented view of it.

If this view of the relationship between the editing of the book of Isaiah and the authors of the Deuteronomic movement is accepted, then a number of illuminating factors emerge. The first of these concerns the importance which is now attached by the book of Deuteronomy to the centralisation of worship at a single sanctuary which Yahweh is to choose. In spite of several attempts to trace an older reference of this demand to some sanctuary other than Jerusalem, no truly clear, or satisfactory, alternative to this interpretation presents itself. Far more convincing is the view that this demand was intended to apply to Jerusalem from the outset and that behind it there lies the long political history of Jerusalem and its association with the Davidic dynasty /9/. Certainly by the time that the Deuteronomistic History came to be written no hesitation existed about openly identifying the sanctuary which the law demanded with Jerusalem (cf. I Kings 11:13 etc.) /10/. Our own investigation into the Josianic Redaction of the book of Isaiah and the origin of the narrative of Jerusalem's deliverance show that a very clear historical and prophetic witness was thought to exist to show why Jerusalem was to be singled out in this fashion. Yahweh had himself "chosen" Jerusalem by establishing his dwelling there (cf. Ps. 76:2) and he had revealed the consequences of this choice by protecting Jerusalem from the Assyrians. We have already pointed out the deep historical tensions and frustrations which arose in respect to this belief in God's choice of a unique dwelling-place as a result of the catastrophes of 598 and 587 B.C. Already the narrative of 2 Kings 20:12-19 shows us an early attempt to deal with these tensions in the light of what happened to Jerusalem in 598.

Even more extensively the theological problem engendered after 587 by such a faith is highlighted in the book of Lamentations /11/ and in the extensive Deuteronomistic editing of the book of Jeremiah, especially in regard to his prophecy concerning the temple (Jer. 7:1-15; 26). If we are correct in recognising the popular rise and flourishing of this remarkable Jerusalem-Zion theology during the reign of Josiah, then we can well understand why it was necessary for Jeremiah to oppose the complacency of those people who kept repeating "the temple of Yahweh, the temple of Yahweh, the temple of Yahweh" (Jer. 7:4). Even more we can see that the main thrust of the original Jeremianic prophecy was a warning that the temple would not save the people (so Jer. 7:4-7). It is the Deuteronomistic editors, in the light of what had actually happened in 587, who have elaborated this into a more forthright declaration that the temple would be destroyed (cf. Jer. 26:9). That Jeremiah should have been thought guilty of high treason for speaking against the city of Jerusalem (cf. Jer. 26:11) shows how fervently the belief in the divine protection of the city had taken hold of many of the people. May we not in fact see in this early Josianic Zion theology a significant factor in the confident, but ill-founded, way in which the kings of Judah reacted to the constraints of outside political pressure? First Josiah, in his ill-judged attempt to prevent the passage of Necho through his land (cf. 2 Chron. 35:20-24), then Jehoiakim by his rebellion against Babylon (2 Kings 24:1), and finally Zedekiah in a further rebellion against Babylon (2 Kings 24:20), were guilty of the most crass and reckless political misjudgements. In the light of historical retrospect it is hard to understand why such catastrophic miscalculations occurred in such close succession. The answer is most readily to be found in the brief summary of Lam. 4:12, which summarises the faith that radiates from the story of Jerusalem's deliverance in 701:

> The kings of the earth did not believe,
>   or any of the inhabitants of the world,
> that foe or enemy could enter
>   the gates of Jerusalem.
>
> (Lam. 4:12; cf. Isa. 29:7)

The Davidic-Zion theology which formed a central aspect of the resurgence of hope and political renewal in Josiah's age had relied too heavily upon the human institutions in which it rejoiced, rather than in the God who lay behind them. Tensions that we now find prominently in evidence in the structure of the Deuteronomistic History are one consequence of this. Another is to be seen in the elaborate way in which the Deuteronomistic editors of Jeremiah have gone about their task.

A second feature of importance for an understanding of the development of the Deuteronomic movement also comes to light from the study of the Isaianic tradition which has been our main concern. This concerns the attitude to the kingship as an institution, which reveals many ambiguous features in the way in which the Deuteronomistic historians have dealt with it /12/. Of over-riding significance is the fact that for the Deuteronomists only members of the Davidic dynasty are held to be eligible as kings of Israel. This limitation must certainly be the primary intention of the formulation set out in the Deuteronomic law of the king (Deut. 17:15ff) /13/. More interesting from the point of view of our concern to trace the manner in which the excessive optimism of the original Davidic-Zion theology had to be modified and restated more cautiously is the fact that the demand that the king should submit himself totally to the demands of the book of law has been introduced secondarily /14/. It has come in in order to define more precisely the responsibilities of the king and to show the way in which his success, or failure, would be determined by his obedience to the book of law (Deut. 17:18-20). This concern with the conditioning effect of the king's obedience to God is precisely the major motif which we have found to be present in the narrative of Hezekiah's sickness (2 Kings 20:1-11). This story has itself been set in its present position as an appendix to the narrative of Jerusalem's deliverance in order to bring out the note of obedient piety which Hezekiah was believed to have displayed. A very similar emphasis upon the necessity for obedience, rather than reliance upon the kingship, is made into the central feature of the Deuteronomistic speech set in the mouth of Samuel (1 Sam. 12:1-25). The king cannot, of himself, guarantee the salvation of the people (so especially v.25).

Yet a third aspect of the Deuteronomic theology is brought into sharper focus by the investigation that we have conducted into the theological developments of Josiah's age. It has been the great service of L. Perlitt, in tracing the rise and significance of Israel's covenant theology /15/, to have shown that this is clearly and decisively a Deuteronomistic creation. It did not have a place in the law book of Deuteronomy, but rather has come in most strongly in the Deuteronomistic account of the reform in Josiah's time (2 Kings 22-23), and in the Deuteronomistic additions to the original law book. Evidently within the early development of the Deuteronomic-Deuteronomistic movement the need arose to find a way of expressing the nature and conditions of the relationship which bound Yahweh to his people Israel. This was found in the concept of a "covenant" (Hebrew berît), by which the terms of Israel's obedience were spelt out. We need not attempt here to re-examine the possible sources of such a covenant theology. What it achieved was a highly distinctive theology which centred around the conviction that the relationship between God and his people was morally and religiously "conditioned" /16/. This is precisely the aspect of the Davidic-Zion theology of Josiah's age which our own examination of its subsequent development history has brought to light. The appending of the two narratives of 2 Kings 20:1-19 to the original story of Jerusalem's deliverance reveals this, as does the Deuteronomistic material in the book of Jeremiah. The fate of Jerusalem as a city, and of the Davidic monarchy, during the reigns of Jehoiakim, Jehoiachin and Zedekiah, show this very clearly. Events themselves had shown that Yahweh did not always defend Jerusalem for "the sake of his servant David" (cf. 2 Kings 19:34; 20:6). The need arose therefore to understand why this was so, if the belief in the special importance of the Davidic dynasty and of the Jerusalem temple was not to be abandoned altogether. The conclusion that a flexible, and "conditioned", relationship existed between Yahweh and Israel would then have been one aspect of the attempt by the Deuteronomic school to deal with this problem. It is not unreasonable to suggest therefore that it was most of all the tension between the original Davidic-Zion theology of Josiah's age and the events of 609, 598 and eventually 587 also, which stimulated the rise of a particular covenant theology in the Deuteronomistic circles.

The raising of these issues points us to consider the wider problem of the present setting of the Isaiah narrative of 2 Kings 18:17-19:37, together with its two appendices in 2 Kings 20:1-19. The date at which the latest of these narratives was composed we have put at no later than Zedekiah's reign (598-587). Together they form a trilogy, and it appears in every way probable that they have been introduced as a connected group of three narratives into their present position between the record of the fall of the Northern Kingdom of Israel and the account of the great reform in Josiah's time. /17/ The intervening history in 2 Kings 21:1-26 is almost entirely taken up with the account of, and comment upon, Manasseh's evil reign, which is used as a kind of preparation for the shock of the report of Jerusalem's eventual fall (so especially 2 Kings 21:10-15). In this there appears more than a hint that even Judah's days are numbered as the remnant of God's heritage (so v.14).

Two problems present themselves for our consideration. The first of these concerns the date of the Deuteronomistic History itself in which our trilogy of narratives is now set. The second is related to, and in some measure dependent upon, the conclusions reached in regard to this, since it concerns the time when our trilogy of narratives was set in the larger work. Neither question can be answered with anything like certainty, but some constructive observations may be made. So far as the date of the Deuteronomistic History as a whole is concerned, M. Noth argued originally for a time circa 550 B.C., probably in Judah /18/. More recently, however, F.M. Cross has adduced some pertinent reasons why the first draft of the History can more plausibly be ascribed to the reign of Josiah, with a subsequent revision and expansion being made to take account of events after this king's death /19/. However, W. Dietrich, who also sees more than one edition of the work, sets the earliest of these after 587, with a DtrN and a DtrP revision being made at intervals after this /20/. He advocates the conclusion that our trilogy of Isaiah narratives was incorporated as part of the last of these revisions (DtrP) /21/. In order to facilitate the resolution of the problems we may note several relevant factors. In addition to the important theological factors which Cross adduces for a Josianic date of the original History we should note also the great importance of the question of the availability of sources. The editor evidently had at his disposal the Chronicles of the kings of Israel, as well as Judah, and a number of important official documents and lists which must have been preserved in the palace library of Jerusalem. It would be most surprising if these important documentary sources had survived the destruction of 587, and, in any case, it is scarcely conceivable that such materials remained readily available after that time. A date for the original draft before 587 is therefore eminently likely. Yet considerations which we have dealt with earlier show that it is impossible that the narrative of the Babylonian emissaries sent to Hezekiah (2 Kings 20:12-19) could have been composed as early as Josiah's time /22/. If we are to hold fast to the conviction that the trilogy of narratives once existed as a separate entity, then this means that the three of them together must have been placed in their present position no earlier than Zedekiah's reign. I have elsewhere suggested that this brief period is by no means as unlikely a time for the composition of the first draft of the Deuteronomistic History, which may in any case have been begun as early as Josiah's reign, as it may first appear /23/. Yet it is not the only possibility. If we were to follow Dietrich's suggestion, that the trilogy of narratives involving the prophet Isaiah belongs to a relatively late revision of the History (DtrP), then this leaves unresolved the enigma of why such a redactor incorporated material which had become obsolete in the wake of events. Even the modified Davidic-Zion theology contained in the trilogy had been shown to be false by what had happened to both Jerusalem and the Davidic monarchy in 587. Alternatively we might conclude that the original narrative concerning Jerusalem's deliverance (2 Kings 18:17-19:37) had been incorporated into the first draft of the Deuteronomistic History, and that it was after this incorporation that the two appendices (2 Kings 20:1-11, 12-19) were added. This is undoubtedly possible, although it breaks up the evident sense of relationship which permeates all three narratives and holds them together. On balance it might appear that the suggestion of the incorporation of all three narratives into the first draft of the Deuteronomistic History during Zedekiah's reign is the most likely explanation.

However, the purely literary problem of tracing the sequence, and most probable date, of the incorporation of the trilogy of "Isaiah" narratives into the Deuteronomistic History is not the most important aspect of the problem of their present setting. More significant is the question of the theological sequence which they display, since there is an evident attempt to demonstrate a major theological position by means of a narrative, and then to modify this by the narration of further incidents. So far as the three "Isaiah" narratives are concerned we have already fully examined their sequence of composition earlier. What is now requisite is some correlation of this sequence with comparable signs of tensions and unevenness in the Deuteronomistic History. Here too it is precisely the questions of the role of Jerusalem-Zion as the religious centre of all Israel and of the Davidic dynasty as the chosen political rulers which hold the centre of attention. The attempt of F.M. Cross to trace two editions of the work largely centres upon the recognition that the major theological positions which run through it in respect of the divine election of Jerusalem and the Davidic dynasty were more or less completely confounded by what happened in 587 /24/. Our trilogy of narratives therefore, with their centre in a highly dogmatic interpretation of the deliverance afforded to Jerusalem in 701, belongs decidedly on the pre-587 side of this editorial work. This holds true for the circles from whom the "Isaiah" narratives originated, but also, although with less certainty, for those editors who incorporated them into the larger work. That this took place during Zedekiah's reign, when the last of the three narratives was added, is the most satisfactory compromise. That this was also the period when the larger work received its essential scope and form appears perfectly reasonable. In any case the importance of the theological positions expressed through the "Isaiah" narratives was fully recognised in the larger History. This is shown by the way in which the "Isaianic" prophecy regarding the fate of the royal treasures of Jerusalem and of its temple (2 Kings 20:17) is alluded to in relation to the events of 598 (2 Kings 24:13). What we find in the Deuteronomistic History, as also in the complex process of literary addition which has produced our present form of the book of Deuteronomy, is an intriguing process of theological debate and development. What, from a purely literary point of view, may appear as a process of piecemeal addition and elaboration, reveals significant underlying theological issues. In a real sense major theological positions were being tested and tried in the fires of historical events. Hence the conclusion that the Deuteronomic-Deuteronomistic movement was active both politically and in literary composition for a period of more than half a century - from early in Josiah's reign until at least the middle of the sixth century - explains the complex literary growth which the writings which we have come to ascribe to it display. A further point may be made in regard to this. The fact that the Deuteronomic writings were not completed as independent and self-contained entities, but underwent a prolonged series of revisions, and appeared in different recensions, makes the claim for a clear-cut distinction between what is "Deuteronomic" and what is better described as "Deuteronomistic" a difficult one to sustain /25/. There is evidently much material in the book of Deuteronomy which must be regarded as Deuteronomistic in its origin. A purely literary application of the adjectives therefore cannot be maintained. A more theologically defined distinction is desirable, but this too is hard to establish with sufficient precision to be of widespread acceptability. The fact that both the book of Deuteronomy as well as the History from Joshua to 2 Kings have undergone a series of additions and elaborations makes any precise theological correlation of such revisions difficult to identify. However we may suggest that one major shift in the theological outlook of the Deuteronomic school can be seen to have taken place with the introduction of a "covenant" theology. The implied element of conditioning, and the intensified emphasis upon obedience to the <u>torah</u> as the way to the achievement of Israel's special destiny, made the introduction of this concept a notable turning-point. Furthermore it appears in every way likely that this new concept, with the element of doubt and uncertainty about the future which it brought with it, was introduced after Josiah's untimely death in 609.

Certainly a further major shift in the theology of the Deuteronomic movement was brought about by the catastrophe of 587, when the two institutions upon which most hope had been centred - the Davidic dynasty and the temple of Jerusalem - suffered the most serious misfortunes. Yet another turning point appears to have been created by the murder of Gedaliah, if we are to judge from the pronounced emphasis which the Deuteronomistic editors of Jeremiah have placed upon the Babylonian exiles as alone remaining the source of hope for the future of Israel /26/. That any single one of these steps in the theological development of the Deuteronomic School marks the

Five: Theological Perspective

transition to a "Deuteronomistic", rather than a "Deutero-nomic", phase in its history cannot be clearly shown. The adjectives therefore remain somewhat relative. However what we can discover of the development of thought within this School shows that it would be mistaken to suppose, as has often been done, that it was the events of the year 587 alone which marked the great crisis of faith for Judah-Israel. Certainly this year witnessed the nadir of Israel's fortunes, but its evils and sufferings were not unanticipated by what had gone before. The very theological vitality and breadth of vision which we can discover in the writings of the Deutero-nomic movement shows that the people of Judah were not overwhelemed in their entirety. There remained a circle of pious thinkers who refused to believe that Yahweh had deserted his people in these sad hours, and who were prepared to re-examine their own theological assumptions and convictions in the light of their historical experience. That they found strength and inspiration in the prophecies of Jeremiah means that this figure was not entirely alone in his preaching of judgement and hope.

In view of the intense convictions regarding Judah and the Davidic dynasty in Yahweh's purposes for Israel which have given theological shape to the final narrative of what took place in 701 B.C., it is surprising that any continuing hope regarding them survived the tragedies of 587. It would appear, on the surface at least, that the Davidic monarchy and the Jerusalem temple had suffered such severe setbacks at the hands of Nebuchadnezzar's soldiers that no credibility in their divine significance could have remained thereafter. Certainly there are strong indications that Jeremiah in particular saw no significant future for the dynasty of David (cf. Jer. 22:28-30), and the same would seem to be true of Ezekiel (Ezek. 19:10-14) /27/. This is clear so far as the hope of restoring the monarchy through Jehoiachin or his descendants was concerned. That Jeremiah was willing to stay in Judah under the governorship of the non-Davidide, Gedaliah (cf. Jer. 40:1-6), also points in this direction. Jeremiah also had, as we have seen, firmly resisted the people's willingness to regard the temple as a guarantee of their security. Ezekiel, even more boldly, had insisted that judgement would first begin at the house of God (cf. Ezek. 9:6). In the aftermath of the exile, however, it is evident that both the Jerusalem temple and the Davidic monarchy retained a large measure of their significance and popular support among those circles who fashioned the hopes and ambitions of those who gave birth to the Judaism of the post-exilic era /28/.

The case of the Davidic monarchy is in some respects the more straight-forward to deal with, since there is now firm documentary evidence in the books of both Jeremiah and Ezekiel that the Davidic monarchy was expected to be restored (Jer. 33:19-26; Ezek. 37:24-28). It is scarcely likely that these prophecies come from those men under whose names they now appear, yet this fact in itself is not of major importance. Nor is it likely that some branch of the Davidic family other than that of Jehoiachin, whose fortunes are no longer known to us, was that upon which these hopes fastened. Every indication points to the growth among the exiles of a belief that Jehoiachin's descendants, if not the ex-king himself, would regain the throne of Judah (cf. 1 Chron. 3:16ff.; Hagg. 2:23) /29/. Deutero-Isaiah appears to have retained a belief in the significance of Yahweh's covenant with the house of David, but to have re-interpreted it in a highly distinctive fashion (Isa. 55:3-5). In the outcome we know that the Davidic monarchy never was restored to the throne of Israel, although the interesting and obscure political developments which surrounded the figure of Zerubbabel towards the end of the fifth century show how strongly the hope that this would happen remained alive. The hope that failed to be realised in the political sense, however, eventually acquired a very remarkable dimension in the later forms of the Jewish messianic hope. Hence the belief that God's actions towards his people Israel were governed by a regard for "his servant David" did not entirely disappear, but eventually took on a novel and influential significance. This aspect of the theology of the narrative of 2 Kings 18:17-19:37 was destined therefore to have a very enduring vitality. Perhaps this has been even more truly the case in regard to the special importance which this narrative attaches to the city of Jerusalem. Of course, the belief that this city was the subject of a special destiny in the election and historical fortunes of Israel did not originate with the composition of this historical narrative. As we have seen, the elements from which this faith was fashioned were complex and varied. Yet it is in this narrative that the faith in Jerusalem's especially privileged position among the cities of Israel reaches a high-point. The city's chequered fortunes after Josiah's reign necessitated a considerable degree of modification to the simplicity of the original assertions.

It is not difficult to see, however, that in spite of all the misfortunes that befell Jerusalem in 598 and 587, the belief that the city held a unique place in the life and destiny of Israel was to play a major part in the restoration of Judaism in the post-exilic period and in the religious life of the Diaspora. For Deutero-Isaiah the rebuilding of the city of Jerusalem, and of its temple in particular, were to be the central features of the life of the restored people of God (Isa. 44:28; 54:11-17). In the words of a later prophet, the very bedrock upon which the hopes and aspirations of the Jewish community was established was the conviction that Yahweh would act "for Zion's sake":

For Zion's sake I will not keep silent,
    and for Jerusalem's sake I will not rest,
until her vindication goes forth as brightness,
    and her salvation as a burning torch.
The nations shall see your vindication,
    and all the kings your glory;
and you shall be called by a new name
    which the mouth of Yahweh will give.
You shall be a crown of beauty in the hand of Yahweh,
    and a royal diadem in the hand of your God.
You shall no more be termed Forsaken,
    and your land shall no more be termed Desolate;
but you shall be called My delight is in her,
    and your land Married;
for Yahweh delights in you,
    and your land shall be married.
For as a young man marries a virgin,
    so shall your sons marry you,
and as the bridegroom rejoices over the bride,
    so shall your God rejoice over you.
      (Isa. 62:1-5; cf. also vv.6-12)

In the situation which came to pertain after the ending of the Babylonian exile, when the hope of restoring a truly independent kingdom of Israel once again under a Davidic king gradually faded, the role of Jerusalem as a symbol and focus of Jewish hope grew rather than diminished. Judaism became the religion of a people in diaspora, and Israel itself became a loosely-defined community of people scattered among many nations. The land, which had once defined the extent of the nation, became the subject of hope and aspiration, rather than the living heritage upon which the nation existed. Yet within this period of political turmoil and trouble, Jerusalem had been regained, its walls rebuilt and its temple restored. Yet it was not simply because the temple stood there that the city remained significant (cf. Isa. 66:1-2; Jer. 3:17), but because the city had itself become a central factor in the faith of Israel. It became a visible embodiment of the concept of Israel's divine election and eventually an eschatological symbol of the final triumphant life of the people of God (cf. Rev. 21:2ff.). No longer was it viewed as a city of stones and bricks, but as a place of peace, prosperity and virtue (cf. Rev. 21:7). As such the confines of the earthly city were transcended and a more spiritualised interpretation of its reality affirmed. Nevertheless it remained the city of God, and an interesting and long historical and theological tradition related it to the city which escaped Sennacherib's vindictive destruction in 701.

Notes to Chapter 1
SENNACHERIB AND JERUSALEM

1 George Smith, History of Sennacherib Translated from the Cuneiform Inscriptions, ed. by A.H. Sayce, London, 1878.
2 Cf. D.D. Luckenbill, The Annals of Sennacherib (Oriental Institute Publications, II), Chicago, 1924. Cf. ANET³, pp.287f.
3 Cf. especially L.L. Honor, Sennacherib's Invasion of Palestine. A Critical Source Study (Contributions to Oriental History and Philology No.12), New York, 1926; B.S. Childs, Isaiah and the Assyrian Crisis (SBT Second Series 3), London, 1967. Further literature is cited in these studies. An extensive bibliography is also to be found in H.H. Rowley, "Hezekiah's Reform and Rebellion", BJRL 44 (1961-2), pp.395-461, reprinted in Men of God. Studies in Old Testament History and Prophecy, London and Edinburgh, 1963, pp.98-132. J. Bright, A History of Israel, 2nd ed., London, 1972, pp.282-7.
4 B.S. Childs, op.cit., p.120
5 Cf. J. Bright, op.cit., pp.286f.
6 ANET³, p.288.
7 L.L. Honor, op.cit., pp.xll-xlv
8 Cf. H.-J. Kraus, Worship in Israel, Eng. Tr. by G. Buswell, Oxford, 1976, pp.181ff.; H.-M. Lutz, Jahwe, Jerusalem und die Völker. Zur Vorgeschichte von Sach. 12, 1-8 und 14,1-5 (WMANT 27) Neukirchen-Vluyn, 1968, pp.33ff.; F. Stolz, Strukturen und Figuren im Kult von Jerusalem. Studien zur altorientalischen Religion (BZAW 118), Berlin, 1970, pp.86ff.; J. Schreiner, Sion-Jerusalem. Jahwes Königsitz. Theologie der heiligen Stadt im Alten Testament (SANT 7), Munich, 1963, pp.217ff. My earlier work, God and Temple. The Idea of the Divine Prescence in Ancient Israel, Oxford, 1965, now requires substantial revision on this subject.
9 Cf. especially A.F. Kirkpatrick, The Book of Psalms (The Cambridge Bible), Cambridge, 1902, p.253: "The miraculous deliverance of Jerusalem from the army of Sennacherib in

the reign of Hezekiah (B.C. 701) may be assigned as the occasion of these Psalms, with a probability which approaches certainty".

10 The different consequences of the two systems of government are well described and noted in M. Cogan, Imperialism and Religion. Assyria, Judah and Israel in the Eighth and Seventh Centuries BCE (SBL Monograph Series 19), Missoula, 1974, pp.65ff.; cf. also H. Donner in Israelite and Judean History, ed. J.H. Hayes and J. Maxwell Miller, London, 1977, pp.415ff.; further comments are to be found in J.W. McKay, Religion in Judah under the Assyrians, 732-609 BC (SBT Second Series 26), London, 1973.

11 H. Donner, op.cit., p.419. M. Cogan, op.cit. p.98, mentions that, after 732, Israel was divided into three Assyrian provinces.

12 M. Cogan, op.cit. pp.65ff.

13 S. Mowinckel, Psalmenstudien II, Oslo, 1921, p.65. It is important, however, to note Mowinckel's indebtedness to H. Gunkel, who had earlier in his Ausgewählte Psalmen (2nd ed., Göttingen, 1905), pp.109-13, argued that Ps. 46 is an eschatological hymn, which draws upon themes and images of a mythological nature in their origin (esp. p.113).

14 G. von Rad, Old Testament Theology, vol.2, Eng. Tr. by D.M.G. Stalker, Edinburgh and London, 1965, pp.155ff.; cf. also his essay, "The City on a Hill", The Problem of the Hexateuch and Other Essays, Eng. Tr. by E.W. Trueman Dicken, Edinburgh and London, 1966, pp.232-42. Cf. also J. Schreiner, Sion-Jerusalem, pp.243ff.

15 Cf. G. von Rad, Old Testament Theology, vol.2, p.147: "The preaching of Isaiah represents the theological high water mark of the whole Old Testament".

16 Cf. G. von Rad, Old Testament Theology, vol.2, p.166: "He [Hezekiah] did not 'show faith', at least not as Isaiah conceived the term, but by an act of political common-sense saved the city from the worst possible fate".

17 E. Troeltsch, "Das Ethos der hebräischen Propheten", Logos 6 (1916), pp.1-28; N.K. Gottwald, All the Kingdoms of the Earth, New York, 1964, pp.355ff.

18 This is basically the position adopted by W. Dietrich, Jesaja und die Politik (BEvTh 74), Munich, 1976, pp.121ff. Dietrich relates the sharp anti-Assyrian sayings of Isaiah to the period 713-711, but concludes that this assurance to

Hezekiah was subsequently changed to an attitude of threat on account of the latter's reliance on his treaty with Egypt.
19 G. Fohrer, Das Buch Jesaja (Zürcher Bibelkommentare), vol.1, Zürich and Stuttgart, 1959; vol.2, 1962. See especially Fohrer's treatment of chapters 36-39 of the book of Isaiah in vol.2, pp.151ff. Cf. also his comment (vol.2, p.157): "The narrative records, not how it was, but how it could and should have been".
20 Cf. D. Bonhoeffer, Letters and Papers from Prison, ed. E. Bethge, Eng. Tr. by R. Fuller et al., 3rd ed., London 1967, pp.195-7. Cf. especially p.196: "God would have us know that we must live as men who manage our lives without him".

Notes to Chapter 2
ISAIAH AND THE THREAT TO JERUSALEM

1 As, for example, J. Schreiner, Sion-Jerusalem. Jahwes Königsitz, pp.236ff., who fully admits the apparent contradictoriness of Isaiah's attitude in condemning Hezekiah's rebellion, but at the same time assuring the king in 701 that Jerusalem would be delivered from the Assyrians. Cf. also J. Bright, Covenant and Promise, p.100.
2 For the more detailed exposition of the passages dealt with reference should be made to my forthcoming commentary on Isaiah 1-39 in the series New Century Bible.
3 Cf. J. Gray, I & II Kings. A Commentary, London, 1964, on the prophecies of 2 Kings 19:21-35: "Probably all these are from Isaiah in the reign of Hezekiah, or from the Isaianic circle, but on the periphery of the authentic Isaianic tradition."
4 Admittedly the translation of the preposition 'al as "against", rather than "upon" (as AV, RSV), is crucial here. Yet it must be argued that it is the more natural rendering in the context and brings the interpretation of 31:4 exactly into line with 29:1-4, thereby establishing a greater consistency in the presentation of the prophet's preaching. Cf. B.S. Childs, Isaiah and the Assyrian Crisis, p.58, who notes parallel occurrences of the phrase "to fight against" (Heb. lisbo' 'al) in Isa. 29:7,8; Num. 31:7 and Zech. 14:12.
5 The passage has been widely related to the Assyrian

advance on Jerusalem in 701. Cf. J. Skinner, Isaiah I-XXXIX, Cambridge, 1913, p.100. However, the fact that Sennacherib advanced on the city from the south, and not from the more readily predictable northern route, has raised doubts regarding this. Hence H. Donner, Israel unter den Völkern (SVT 11), 1964, pp.31ff., has argued that it can better be related to the Syro-Ephraimite advance on the city in 735. More recently still D.L. Christensen, "The March of Conquest in Isaiah x 27c-34", VT 26 (1976), pp.385-399, has argued that an even more complex, and partly mythological, tradition lies behind the portrayal of the advance. However, the literary context, both in what precedes in Isa. 10:20-27a, and in what follows in vv.33-4, strongly suggests a relationship to Judah's conflict with Assyria. This would strongly support the contention that the undefined "he" of 10:27b refers to the Assyrians. That Isaiah should have visualised the route of the Assyrian attack being from the north, although in the event, this was not the one that the advancing army took, scarcely invalidates it as genuine prophecy. The prophet was concerned to stress the certainty, not the strategy, of the Assyrian suppression of Hezekiah's defection.

6   So J. Schreiner, Sion-Jerusalem. Jahwes Königsitz, pp.267-9. By placing the prophecies of assurance to Hezekiah in the period 713-711, W. Dietrich, Jesaja und die Politik, pp.113ff., endeavours to maintain their authenticity to Isaiah, without weakening the note of threat in the years 705-701. Dietrich thinks to discover a change of attitude on the prophet's part, engendered by Hezekiah's lack of faith. This latter found its major expression in the conclusion of the treaty with Egypt.

7   So J. Skinner, Isaiah I-XXXIX, pp.276ff.; H.H. Rowley, "Hezekiah's Reform and Rebellion", pp.99ff.

8   Cf. my commentary in loc.

9   Cf. H. Barth, Die Jesaja-Worte, p.190.

10 H. Barth, Die Jesaja-Worte, pp.141ff.

11 A. Alt, "Jesaja 8,23-9,6. Befreiungsnacht und Krönungstag", Festschrift A. Bertholet zum 80. Geburtstag, Tübingen, 1950, pp.29-49 = Kleine Schriften, II, Munich, 1953, pp.206-225.

12 S.R. Driver, Isaiah. His Life and Times, London, 1888, p.75.

13 G. von Rad, Old Testament Theology, vol. 2, Eng. Tr. by

D. Stalker, Edinburgh, 1965, pp.147ff.; J. Schreiner, Sion-Jerusalem. Jahwes Königsitz, pp.243ff.
14   Cf. H. Barth, Die Jesaja-Worte, pp.28ff.
15   Cf. H. Barth, Die Jesaja-Worte, passim.
16   Cf. H. Barth, Die Jesaja-Worte, pp.35ff., 43ff.

Notes to Chapter 3
THE ISAIAH NARRATIVES

1   The literary structure of the narratives, and their relationship to the books of 1 and 2 Kings, are examined by J. Meinhold, Die Jesajaerzählungen. Jesaja 36-39. Eine historisch-kritische Untersuchung, Göttingen, 1898. Cf. also O. Kaiser, Isaiah 13-39. A Commentary. Eng. Tr. by R.A. Wilson, London, 1974.
2   Cf. B.S. Childs, Isaiah and the Assyrian Crisis, pp.69ff.
3   B. Stade, "Miscellen: Anmerkungen zu 2 Kö. 15-21", ZAW 6 (1886), pp.156-89, esp. pp.172-8.
4   Cf. J. Skinner, Isaiah I-XXXIX, pp.277f.
5   This Tirhakah became ruler of Upper and Lower Egypt in 690/689, whereas Hezekiah died at the latest in 697/696. The mention of Tirhakah has been used to support the claim that Sennacherib mounted a second campaign in the west, which involved Judah, after 701, and perhaps as late as 689-688. Such a view goes back to G. Rawlinson, The History of Herodotus, I, 1858; see H.H. Rowley, "Hezekiah's Reform and Rebellion", p.107 note 3.
6   Sennacherib died in 681, and there is no independent corroboration from Assyrian sources of the manner of his death. Nevertheless no reasons exist for doubting the accuracy of this biblical report of it.
7   The history of Tirhakah has now been dealt with extensively by K.A. Kitchen, The Third Intermediate Period in Egypt (1100-650 B.C.), Warminster, 1973, pp.154-72, 387-93. Cf. also J.M.A. Janssen, "Que sait-on actuellement du Pharaon Taharqa?", Biblica 34 (1953), pp.23-43.
8   The B2 account is set out by B.S. Childs, Isaiah and the Assyrian Crisis, pp.94-6. While I am in general agreement with Childs' overall analysis, this ought not to preclude the recognition that within the narrative that is thereby isolated

the material may be from more than one author. This especially applies to the Isaianic "prophecies" of 2 Kings 19:21-34, where it is evident that a substantial expansion has taken place. Cf. O. Kaiser, Isaiah 13-39, pp.376f.

9   For this Deuteronomic polemic against the worship of other gods, cf. E. Rössler, Jahwe und die Götter im Pentateuch und im deuteronomistischen Geschichtswerk (Diss. Bonn, 1966, pp.165ff.). For the vocabulary employed cf. M. Weinfeld, Deuteronomy and the Deuteronomic School, Oxford, 1972, Appendix A, pp.320-24. Further material is to be found in H.D. Preuss, Verspottung fremder Religionen im Alten Testament (BWANT V:12), Stuttgart-Berlin-Cologne-Mainz, 1971, pp.141ff.

10   Cf. O. Kaiser, Isaiah 13-39, p.376.

11   We have already pointed out the unsatisfactoriness of attempts to rationalise the reference to the activity of the angel of Yahweh by relating it to an outbreak of plague. Cf. H.H. Rowley, "Hezekiah's Reform and Rebellion", p.125; J. Bright, A History of Israel, p.283. The mention by Herodotus, Bk. II, 141, that Sennacherib's army was overrun by mice has frequently been cited in further support of such a conclusion, but scarcely adds much weight to such rationalisations.

12   The annals of Sennacherib certainly suggest that the battle at Eltekeh, in which the Egyptians were defeated, had already taken place before the attack on Judah began (cf. ANET, p.287). However the evidence may not be entirely clear since it is possible that the annals do not follow a precise chronological sequence, but refer to Assyria's enemies in some geographically determined order.

13   That this verse in Hos. 1:7 is a gloss is widely recognised. Cf. H.W.Wolff, Hosea (Hermeneia), Eng. Tr. by G. Stansell, Philadelphia, 1974, pp.20f., who rightly places it before 587 B.C. Contrast I. Willi-Plein, Vorformen der Schriftexegese innerhalb des Alten Testaments (BZAW 123), Berlin - New York, 1971, p.117, who ascribes it to a late post-exilic date.

14   For these two narratives see especially P.R. Ackroyd, "An Interpretation of the Babylonian Exile: A Study of 2 Kings 20, Isaiah 38-39", SJT 27 (1974), pp.329-52, and my essay, "The Isaiah Narrative of 2 Kings 20,12-19 and the Date of the Deuteronomic History", Studies in Ancient Narrative and Historiography (I.L. Seeligman Anniversary Volume), ed. A. Rofé and Y. Zakovitch, Jerusalem, 1979).

15 We may notice the introduction of a similar note of conditional promise in regard to the divine support for the Davidic monarchy in Ps. 132:12. Furthermore the emphasis upon the need for obedience to the written torah on the part of the king in Deut. 17:18-19 must be recognised as deriving from a late addition to the Deuteronomic legislation. Cf. G. von Rad, Deuteronomy. A Commentary, Eng. Tr. by D.M. Barton, London, 1966, p.119.

16 J. Gray, I and II Kings, London, 1964, pp.633, 637, prefers a date in the period 714-709, perhaps 711 B.C.; P.R. Ackroyd, art. cit. p.331, prefers a date ca. 703.

17 Cf. the discussion of this point in my article referred to in note 14 above.

18 Additional reasons why Zedekiah's reign may be regarded as an important one for some of the literary developments of the Deuteronomic movement, especially in regard to the editing of the book of Jeremiah are noted in the above mentioned article.

19 The thesis proposed by S. Mowinckel in his study Jesaja-Disiplene. Profetien fra Jesaja til Jeremia, Oslo, 1926, pp.10ff., is attractive on account of its drawing together certain significant similarities of thought and language which are to be found in Isaiah 1-39, the Zion hymns of the Psalter and the book of Deuteronomy. Yet the thesis that these literary and theological connections are all to be explained as the work of "Isaiah's disciples" is to resort to a quite unproven hypothesis about the aims of such a literary circle. Their interests were evidently very strongly attached to Jerusalem and the royal Davidic court.

20 Cf. G. von Rad, Old Testament Theology, vol. 1, pp.341ff.

Notes to Chapter 4
ISAIAH AND THE ZION TRADITION

1 G. von Rad, Old Testament Theology, vol. 1, p.149.
2 S. Mowinckel, Psalmenstudien II, Oslo, 1921, p.65.
3 S. Mowinckel, Jesaja-Disiplene, pp.10ff.
4 H. Gunkel, art. "Die Psalmen" in RGG, 1st ed., Göttingen, 190; cf. The Psalms. A Form-Critical Introduction (Facet Books 19), Eng. Tr. by T.M. Horner, Philadelphia,

1967, p.31; also H. Gunkel-J. Begrich, Einleitung in die Psalmen, 2nd ed., Göttingen, 1966, p.145.
5 A.F. Kirkpatrick, The Psalms (The Cambridge Bible), Cambridge, 1902, p.253.
6 H. Gunkel, Ausgewählte Psalmen, 2nd ed., Göttingen, 1905, p.110.
7 E. Rohland, Die Bedeutung der Erwählungstraditionen Israels für die Eschatologie der alttestamentlichen Propheten, Diss. Heidelberg, 1956, esp. pp.145ff.
8 H.-J. Kraus, Worship in Israel. A Cultic History of the Old Testament, Eng. Tr. by G. Buswell, Oxford, 1966, pp.183ff. Cf. also J.H. Hayes, "The Tradition of Zion's Inviolability", JBL 82 (1963), pp.419-26.
9 A.R. Johnson, Sacral Kingship in Ancient Israel, 2nd ed., Cardiff, 1967, pp.31ff.; J. Schreiner, Sion-Jerusalem. Jahwes Königsitz, p.10; F. Stolz, Strukturen und Figuren im Kult von Jerusalem, p.90.
11 E. Rohland, op.cit. pp.145ff.; G. Wanke, Die Zionstheologie der Korachiten in ihrem traditionsgeschichtlichen Zusammenhang (BZAW 97), Berlin, 1966, pp.70ff., attempts to place the whole "Zion theology", along with the Zion psalms from which it has been drawn, to a late, post-exilic, period. Cf. also G. Fohrer, "Zion-Jerusalem im Alten Testament", Studien zur alttestamentlichen Theologie und Geschichte (1949-1966) (BZAW 115), Berlin, 1969, pp.195-241.
12 H. Wildberger, "Die Völkerwallfahrt zum Zion. Jes. ii 1-5", VT (1957), pp.62-81; idem, Jesaja 1-12, pp.75ff.
13 Cf. especially J.J.M. Roberts, "The Davidic Origin of the Zion tradition", JBL 92 (1973), pp.329-344.
14 F. Stolz, Strukturen und Figuren im Kult von Jerusalem, esp. pp.86ff.
15 Cf. O. Kaiser, Die mythische Bedeutung des Meeres in Ägypten, Ugarit und Israel (BZAW 78), Berlin, 1959.
16 Cf. my God and Temple, pp.71f.
17 Cf. R. Rendtorff, "El, Baal und Jahwe", ZAW 78 (1966), pp.177-92 = Ges. Stud. zum A.T. (ThB 57), Munich, 1975, pp.172-87.
18 Cf. K. Rupprecht, Der Tempel von Jerusalem. Gründung Salomos oder jebusitisches Erbe? (BZAW 144), Berlin-New York, 1977.
19 This point is stressed quite heavily by J.A. Soggin, "Der offiziell geförderte Synkretismus in Israel während des 10.

Jahrhunderts", ZAW 78 (1966), pp.179-204; cf. also G.W. Ahlstrom, Aspects of Syncretism in Israelite Religion, Uppsala, 1963. Cf. also H.-J. Kraus, Exkurs 4, "Die Kulttraditionen Jerusalems", in Die Psalmen (BKAT XV, 10), vol. 1, Neukirchen, 1960, pp.197-205.
20 H.M. Lutz, Jahwe, Jerusalem und die Völker, pp. 175-6.
21 J.J.M. Roberts, op.cit. pp.338f.
22 Cf. H. Gunkel, Die Psalmen, 5th ed., Göttingen, 1968, pp.5ff.; The Psalms. A Form-Critical Introduction, p.24.
23 Cf. J. Bright, Covenant and Promise, p.55.
24 Cf. N. Poulssen, König und Tempel im Glaubenszeugnis des Alten Testamentes (SBM 3), Stuttgart, 1967, pp.87ff.
25 Cf. J.A. Soggin, Das Königtum in Israel. Ursprünge, Spannungen, Entwicklung (BZAW 104), Berlin, 1967, pp.115ff.
26 Cf. T.N.D. Mettinger, King and Messiah, pp.259ff.
27 Cf. G. von Rad, "The Royal Ritual in Judah", The Problem of the Hexateuch and Other Essays, pp.222-31.
28 Cf. T.N.D. Mettinger, Solomonic State Officials. A Study of the Civil Government Officials of the Israelite Monarchy (Coniectanea Biblica: Old Testament Series 5), Lund, 1971, pp.25ff.; R. de Vaux, Ancient Israel. Its Life and Institutions, Eng. Tr. by J. McHugh, London, 1961, pp.127-32.
29 Cf. P.J. Calderone, Dynastic Oracle and Suzerainty Treaty. 2 Samuel 7,8-16, Manila, 1966, pp.41ff.
30 Cf. H.-J. Kraus, Worship in Israel, pp.181, 205.
31 Cf. above note 6.
32 Cf. above p.41f.
33 Cf. above p.40.
34 In this conclusion I differ from the views expressed most recently, for example, by J. Bright, Covenant and Promise, pp.78ff.
35 Cf. J. Bright, Covenant and Promise. pp.126ff., especially the comment on p.128: "Reform was a facet of independence and nationalism".
36 Cf. S. Mowinckel, The Psalms in Israel's Worship, Eng. Tr. by D.R. Ap-Thomas, vol. 1, Oxford, 1962, pp.181ff.
37 Cf. A. Malamat, "Josiah's Bid for Armageddon. The Background of the Judean Egyptian Encounter in 609 B.C.", The Gaster Festschrift. The Journal of the Ancient Near Eastern Society of Columbia University, vol. 5 (1973), pp.167-78.
38 Cf. J. Bright, Covenant and Promise, pp.196f.

Notes to Chapter 5
THE DELIVERANCE OF JERUSALEM
IN THEOLOGICAL PERSPECTIVE

1   Cf. my earlier work God's Chosen People. A Theological
Interpretation of the Book of Deuteronomy, London, 1968; a
much fuller treatment is now to be found in M. Weinfeld,
Deuteronomy and the Deuteronomic School, Oxford, 1972.
2   This position agrees in considerable measure with the
assessment of the historical situation given by S. Mowinckel,
cited above p.71, and with the historical conclusions which lie
at the basis of the interpretations offered by G. Fohrer and
G. von Rad. However, I have presented above a very different view and interpretation of the preaching of Isaiah from
that offered by each of these scholars. This is also true in
respect of the work of W. Dietrich, noted above pp.32, 111,
with whose historical conclusions regarding what happened in
701 I substantially concur. However, his understanding of the
content of Isaiah's preaching, especially in regard to the
so-called "anti-Assyrian" prophecies, differs considerably
from the explanations set out above.
3   See above p.41f.
4   See above p.114 note 19.
5   The prominence of this "Remnant Theology", which is
based upon later interpretations placed upon the name of
Isaiah's child Shear-jashub (Isa. 7:2), is revealed by the
extensive use made of it in the redaction of the book of
Isaiah. Cf. especially Isa. 10:20-23 and 2 Kings 19:30-31. See
H. Barth, Die Jesaja-Worte in der Josiazeit, pp.37-41, and H.
Wildberger, article "Sh-'-r" in ThHAT, vol.2, cols.844-55.
However, against Wildberger, op.cit., cols. 853f., who
ascribes it to the post-exilic age, this redactional
development of the name of the prophet's son may be placed
in Josiah's time.
6   For the royal elements in the Deuteronomic movement,
cf. my God's Chosen People, pp.102ff.
7   Cf. above pp.69f. note.
8   As argued especially by G. von Rad, Studies in
Deuteronomy (SBT 9), London, 1953, pp.60ff., and more

recently by J. Lindblom, Erwägungen zur Herkunft der Josianischen Tempelurkunde (Scripta Minora 1970-71:3), Lund, 1971, pp.22ff.
9 Cf. my God's Chosen People, pp.74ff.
10 The attempt of R. de Vaux, "Le lieu que Yahwé a choisi pour y etablir son nom", Das nahe und ferne Wort. L. Rost Festschrift (BZAW 105), Berlin, 1967, pp.219-28, to make a distinction in this regard between the view of the original authors of Deuteronomy and those who later composed the Deuteronomic History (Jos.-2 Kings), cannot be regarded as convincing.
11 Cf. B. Albrektson, Studies in the Text and Theology of the Book of Lamentations, Lund, 1963, pp.214ff.
12 Cf. G. von Rad, Old Testament Theology, vol.1, pp. 334ff.; F. Crüsemann, Der Widerstand gegen das Königtum. Die antiköniglichen Texten des Alten Testamentes und der Kampf um den frühen israelitischen Staat (WMANT 49), Neukirchen-Vluyn, 1978, pp.19ff.; see also my article, "The Deuteronomic Interpretation of the Founding of the Monarchy in 1 Sam. viii", VT 24 (1974), pp.398-410.
13 Cf. my God's Chosen People, pp.46ff.
14 Cf. G. von Rad, Deuteronomy. A Commentary, Eng. Tr. by D.M. Barton, London, 1966, p.119.
15 L. Perlitt, Die Bundestheologie im Alten Testament (WMANT 36), Neukirchen-Vluyn, 1969, pp.54ff.
16 In spite of Perlitt's arguments in the reverse direction it seems to me very probable that the terminology of "covenant" had been current in Israel's political theology earlier than the time of the Deuteronomists. Most probably this was in relation to the ideology of the Davidic monarchy, as shown by 2 Sam. 23:5. This is against Perlitt, op.cit., pp.50-52, who sees here a post-Deuteronomistic revision.
17 Cf. my article, "The Isaiah Narrative of 2 Kings 20:12-19 and the Date of the Deuteronomic History", referred to above (p.114 note 14).
18 M. Noth, Überlieferungsgeschichtliche Studien I, Halle, 1943, repr. Tübingen, 1957, p.110 note 1.
19 F.M. Cross, Canaanite Myth and Hebrew Epic, Cambridge, Mass., 1973, pp.287ff.
20 W. Dietrich, Prophetie und Geschichte (FRLANT 108), Göttingen, 1972, pp.134ff. The tracing of a DtrN and a DtrP is argued by R. Smend, "Das Gesetz und die Völker. Ein

Beitrag zur deuteronomistischen Redaktionsgeschichte", Probleme biblische Theologie. G. von Rad Festschrift 70. Geburtstag, Munich, 1971, pp.494-509.

21 W. Dietrich, Prophetie und Geschichte, p.143, who places the original composition (DtrG) between 587 and 580, with a subsequent prophetic redaction (DtrP), followed by a nomistic redaction (DtrN) in about 560.

22 Cf. my article cited above (note 17).

23 Cf. ibid.

24 Cf. F.M. Cross, "The Structure of the Deuteronomic History", Perspectives in Jewish Learning, Chicago, 1970, pp.9-23; idem, Canaanite Myth and Hebrew Epic, pp.287-90.

25 The original description of the editing of the books Joshua - 2 Kings as "Deuteronomistic" would appear to go back to J. Wellhausen, Prolegomena to the History of Ancient Israel (originally published as History of Israel, I), repr. New York, 1959, pp.231ff.

26 So especially Jer. 24:1-10; 29:1-14. Cf. S. Herrmann, Die prophetische Heilserwartungen im Alten Testament. Ursprung und Gestaltwandel (BWANT V:5), Stuttgart, 1965, pp.188ff.

27 Cf. M. Noth, "The Jerusalem Catastrophe of 587 B.C. and its Significance for Israel", The Laws of the Pentateuch and Other Essays, Eng. Tr. by D.R. Ap-Thomas, Edinburgh-London, 1965, pp.214ff.

28 S. Herrmann, Die prophetische Heilserwartungen im Alten Testament, pp.210ff.

29 Cf. E. Zenger, "Die deuteronomistische Interpretation der Rehabilitierung Jojachins", BZ (NF) 12 (1968), pp.16-30.

BIBLIOGRAPHY

A. Alt, "Jerusalems Aufstieg", ZDMG 79 (1925), pp.1-19 = Kleine Schriften, III, pp.243-57.

"Die territorialgeschichtliche Bedeutung von Sanheribs Eingriff in Palästina", PJB 25 (1930), pp.80-88 = Kleine Schriften, II, pp.242-49.

"Neue Assyrische Nachrichten über Palästina" ZDPV 67 (1945), pp.128-146 = Kleine Schriften II, pp.226-41.

"Jesaja 8,23-9,6. Befreiungsnacht und Krönungstag", Festschrift Alfred Bertholet zum 80. Geburtstag gewidmet, Tübingen, 1950, pp.29-49 = Kleine Schriften, II, pp.206-25.

"Das System der Assyrischen Provinzen auf dem Boden des Reiches Israel", ZDPV 52 (1929), pp.220-42 = Kleine Schriften, II, pp.188-205.

H. Barth, Die Jesaja-Worte in der Josiazeit. Israel und Assur als Thema einer produktiven Neuinterpretation der Jesajaüberlieferung (WMANT 48), Neukirchen-Vluyn, 1978.

J. Begrich, "Der Syrisch-Ephraimitische Krieg und seine weltpolitischen Zusammenhänge", Gesammelte Studien zum Alten Testament, ed. W. Zimmerli (ThB 21), Munich, 1964, pp.99-120.

"Jesaja 14,28-32", Gesammelte Studien zum Alten Testament, pp.121-31.

J. Bright, A History of Israel, 2nd ed., London, 1972.

Covenant and Promise. The Future in the Preaching of the Pre-exilic Prophets, London, 1977.

K. Budde, Jesajas Erleben. Eine gemeinverständliche Auslegung der Denkschrift des Propheten (Kap. 6,1-9,6), Gotha, 1928.

"Jesaja und Ahaz", ZDMG 84 (N.F. 9), 1930, pp.125-38.

B.S. Childs, Isaiah and the Assyrian Crisis (SBT II/3), London, 1967.

R.E. Clements, God's Chosen People. A Theological Interpretation of the Book of Deuteronomy, London, 1968.

M. Cogan, Imperialism and Religion. Assyria, Judah and Israel in the Eighth and Seventh Centuries BCE (SBL Monograph Series 19), Missoula, 1974.

Isaiah and the Deliverance of Jerusalem

F.M. Cross, Canaanite Myth and Hebrew Epic. Essays in the History of the Religion of Israel, Cambridge, Mass., 1973.

W. Dietrich, Prophetie und Geschichte. Eine redaktionsgeschichtliche Untersuchung zum deuteronomistischen Geschichtswerk (FRLANT 108), Göttingen, 1972.

Jesaja und die Politik (BEvTh 74), Munich, 1976.

H. Donner, Israel unter den Völken. Die Stellung der klassischen Propheten des 8. Jahrhunderts v. Chr. zur Aussenpolitik der Könige von Israel (SVT 11), Leiden, 1964

"The Separate States of Israel and Judah", Israelite and Judean History, ed. J.H. Hayes and J. Maxwell Miller, London, 1977, pp.381-434.

W. Eichrodt, Der Heilige in Israel. Jesaja 1-12 (Die Botschaft des A.T.), Zurich, 1960.

Der Herr der Geschichte. Jesaja 13-23 und 28-39 (Die Botschaft des A.T.), Zurich, 1967.

K. Elliger, "Prophet und Politik", Kleine Schriften zum Alten Testament (ThB 32), ed. H. Gese and O. Kaiser, Munich, 1966, pp.119-40.

G. Fohrer, Das Buch Jesaja I. Kap.1-23, 2nd ed., Zurich-Stuttgart, 1966.

Das Buch Jesaja II. Kap.24-29, 2nd ed., Zurich-Stuttgart, 1967.

"Zion-Jerusalem im Alten Testament", Studien zur alttestamentlichen Theologie und Geschichte (1949-1966) (BZAW 115), Berlin, 1969, pp.195-241.

"Die Struktur der alttestamentlichen Eschatologie", Studien zur alttestamentlichen Prophetie (1949-1965) (BZAW 99), 1967, pp.32-58.

"Jesaja 1 als Zusammenfassung der Verkündigung Jesajas", Studien zur alttestamentlichen Prophetie (1949-1965), pp.149-66.

J. Fichtner, "Jahwes Plan in der Botschaft des Jesaja", Gottes Weisheit. Gesammelte Studien zum Alten Testament, ed. K.D. Fricke (Arbeiten zur Theologie II:3), 1965, pp.27-43.

"Die Umkehrung in der prophetischen Botschaften. Eine Studie zu dem Verhältnis von Schuld und Gesicht in der Verkündigung Jesajas", Gottes Weisheit, pp.44-51.

K. Fullerton, "Isaiah's Attitude in the Sennacherib Campaign", AJSL 42 (1925-6), pp.1-25.

H. Gese, "Der Davidsbund und die Zionserwählung", ZThK N.F. 61 (1964), pp.10-26 = Vom Sinai zum Zion. Alttestamentliche Beiträge zur biblischen Theologie (BEvTh 64),

Bibliography

Munich, 1974, pp.113-29.

"Natus ex Virgine", Probleme biblischer Theologie. Gerhard von Rad zum 70. Geburtstag, ed. H.W. Wolff, Munich, 1971, pp.73-89 = Vom Sinai zum Zion, pp.130-46.

G.B. Gray, Isaiah I-XXVII (I.C.C.), Edinburgh, 1912.

A.H.G. Gunneweg, "Hells- und Unheilsverkündigung in Jes. vii", VT 15 (1965), pp.27-34.

H. Haag, "La campagne de Sennacherib contre Jérusalem en 701", RB 58 (1951), pp.348-59.

G.F. Hasel, The Remnant. The History and Theology of the Remnant Idea from Genesis to Isaiah (Andrews University Monographs. Studies in Religion, vol. V), Berrien Springs, 2nd ed., 1974.

S. Herrmann, Die prophetischen Heilserwartungen im Alten Testament. Ursprung und Gestaltwandel (BWANT V:5), Stuttgart, 1965.

H.W. Hoffmann, Die Intention der Verkündigung Jesajas (BZAW 136), Berlin, 1974.

L.L. Honor, Sennacherib's Invasion of Palestine. A Critical Source Study (Contributions to Oriental History and Philology No.12), New York, 1926.

F. Huber, Jahwe, Juda und die anderen Völker beim Propheten Jesaja (BZAW 137), Berlin - New York, 1976.

W.A. Irwin, "The Attitude of Isaiah in the Crisis of 701", Journal of Religion 16 (1936), pp.406-18.

E. Jenni, Die politischen Voraussagen der Propheten (AThANT 29), Zurich, 1956.

O. Kaiser, Isaiah 1 12. A Commentary, Eng. Tr. by R. A. Wilson, London, 1969.

Isaiah 13-39. A Commentary, Eng. Tr. by R. A. Wilson, London.

C.A. Keller, "Das quietistische Element in der Botschaft des Jesaja", ThZ 11 (1955), pp.81-97.

R. Kilian, Die Verheissung Immanuels. Jes.7,14 (SBS 35), Stuttgart, 1968.

H.-J. Kraus, Worship in Israel. A Cultic History of the Old Testament, Eng. Tr. by G. Buswell, Oxford, 1966.

C. van Leeuwen, "Sanchérib devant Jérusalem", Oudtestamentische Studiën XIV, Leiden, 1965, pp.245-72.

J. Lindblom, A Study of the Immanuel Section in Isaiah. Isa. vii,1-ix,9, Lund, 1958.

123

Isaiah and the Deliverance of Jerusalem

H.-M. Lutz, Jahwe, Jerusalem und die Völker. Zur Vorgeschichte von Sach. 12,1-8 und 14,1-5 (WMANT 27), Neukirchen-Vluyn, 1968.

D.D. Luckenbill, The Annals of Sennacherib (Oriental Institute Publications, II), Chicago, 1924.

H.G. Mitchell, "Isaiah on the Fate of His People and the Capital", JBL 37 (1918), pp.149-62.

S. Mowinckel, The Psalms in Israel's Worship, Eng. Tr. by D.R. Ap-Thomas, 2 vols., Oxford, 1962.

M. Noth, "David and Israel in II Samuel vii", The Laws in the Pentateuch and Other Studies, Eng. Tr. by D.R. Ap-Thomas, Edinburgh-London, 1966, pp.250-59.

"Jerusalem and the Israelite Tradition", The Laws in the Pentateuch, pp.132-44.

"The Jerusalem Catastrophe of 587 B.C. and its Significance for Israel", The Laws in the Pentateuch, pp.260-80.

A.L. Oppenheim, "Sennacherib", The Interpreter's Dictionary of the Bible, IV, p.272.

H.M. Orlinsky, "The Kings-Isaiah Recensions of the Hezekiah Story", JQR 30 (1939-40), pp.33-49.

L. Perlitt, Bundestheologie im Alten Testament (WMANT 36), Neukirchen-Vluyn, 1969.

N.W. Porteous, "Jerusalem-Zion. The Growth of a Symbol", Living the Mystery, Oxford, 1967, pp.93-111.

G. von Rad, Old Testament Theology, Eng. Tr. by D.M.G. Stalker, 2 vols., Edinburgh-London, 1962, 1965.

"The City on a Hill", The Problem of the Hexateuch and Other Essays, Eng. Tr. by E.W.T. Dicken, Edinburgh-London, 1965, pp.232-42.

R.W. Rogers, "Sennacherib and Judah", Studien zur semitischen Philologie und Religionsgeschichte. J. Wellhausen Festschrift (BZAW 27), ed. K. Marti, Giessen, 1914, pp.317-28.

E. Rohland, Die Bedeutung der Erwählungstraditionen Israels für die Eschatologie der alttestamentlichen Propheten, Diss. Heidelberg, 1956.

H.H. Rowley, Worship in Ancient Israel. Its Form and Meaning, London, 1967.

"Hezekiah's Reform and Rebellion", BJRL 44 (1961-2), pp.395-461 = Men of God. Studies in Old Testament History and Prophecy, London and Edinburgh, 1963, pp.98-132.

W. Rudolph, "Sanherib in Palästina", PJB 25 (1929),

Bibliography

pp.59-80.
  K. Rupprecht, Der Tempel von Jerusalem. Gründung Salomos oder jebusitisches Erbe? (BZAW 144), Berlin - New York 1977.
  H.H. Schmid, "Jahwe und die Kulttraditionen von Jerusalem", ZAW 67 (1955), pp.168-97.
  J. Schreiner, Sion-Jerusalem. Jahwes Königsitz. Theologie der heiligen Stadt im Alten Testament (SANT 7), Munich, 1963.
  J. Skinner, Isaiah I-XXXIX (The Cambridge Bible), Cambridge, 1913.
  J.A. Soggin, Das Königtum in Israel. Ursprünge, Spannungen, Entwicklung (BZAW 104), Berlin, 1967.
  G. Sauer, "Die Umkehrforderung in der Verkündigung Jesajas", Wort-Gebot-Glaube. W. Eichrodt zum 80. Geburtstag. ed. J.J. Stamm, E. Jenni, H.-J. Stoebe (AThANT 59), Zurich, 1970, pp.277-96.
  B. Stade, "Miscellen", ZAW 4 (1884), pp.250-77.
  U. Stegemann, "Der Restgedanke bei Isaias", BZ (N.F.) 13 (1969), pp.161-86.
  F. Stolz, Strukturen und Figuren im Kult von Jerusalem. Studien zur altorientalischen vor- und frühisraelitischen Religion (BZAW 118), Berlin, 1970.
  R. de Vaux, "Jerusalem and the Prophets", Interpreting the Prophetic Tradition, ed. H.M. Orlinsky, Cincinnati, 1969, pp.275-300.
  J. Vermeylen, Du prophète Isaïe à l'apocalyptique. Isaïe 1 xxxv, miroir d'un demi-millénaire d'expérience religieuse en Israël, 2 vols, Paris, 1978.
  J. Vollmer, "Zur Sprache von Jesaja 9,1-6", ZAW 80 (1968), pp.343-350.
  Th. C. Vriezen, "Essentials of the Theology of Isaiah", Israel's Prophetic Heritage, ed. B.W. Anderson and W. Harrelson, London, 1962, pp.128-46.
  Jahwe en zijn stad, Amsterdam, 1962.
  G. Wanke, Die Zionstheologie der Korachiten (BZAW 97), Berlin 1966.
  H.M. Wiener, "Isaiah and the Siege of Jerusalem", Journal for Study of Religion 11 (1927). pp.195-209.
  H. Wildberger, Jesaja 1-12 (BKAT X,1), Neukirchen-Vluyn, 1972.
  Jesaja 13-27 (BKAT X,2), Neukirchen-Vluyn, 1978.

"Jesajas Verständnis der Geschichte", Bonn Congress Volume (SVT 9), Leiden, 1963, pp.83-117.

"Die Völkerwallfahrt zum Zion", VT 7 (1957), pp.62-81.

E. Würthwein, "Jesaja 7,1-9. Ein Beitrag zum Thema: Prophetie und Politik", Wort und Existenz. Studien zum Alten Testament, Göttingen, 1970, pp.127-43.

W. Zimmerli, "Jesaja und Hiskia", Studien zur alttestamentlichen Theologie und Prophetie. Gesammelte Aufsätze II (ThB 51), Munich, 1974, pp.88-103.

"Verkündigung und Sprache der Botschaft Jesajas", Studien zur alttestamentlichen Theologie und Prophetie, pp.73-87.

INDEX OF BIBLICAL REFERENCES